Universal Freedom

Elios: Universal Freedom –
Advaita Vedanta in the Life Practice
of the 21st Century

Translation: Vidya Bolz
Proof Reading: Robert Regan
Coverdesign/typesetting:
Wilfried Klei
Coverpicture: © photocase – jarts

info@tao.de | www.tao.de

1st edition 2015

Bibliographic information published by the Deutsche Nationalbibliothek
The German National Library lists this publication in the Deutsche Nationalbibliografie; detailed bibliographic data are available under the following internet address: **http://dnb.d-nb.de**.

ISBN Paperback: 978-3-95529-340-6
ISBN Hardcover: 978-3-95529-341-3
ISBN E-Book: 978-3-95529-342-0

Elios
Universal Freedom

Advaita Vedanta In the Life Practice of the 21st Century

Translation from German
Vidya Bolz

tao.de

With pure heart

and in deepest humility

I thank my

Master Raphael

for His presence within and

for His wise guidance

Prologue

In the year of 2006 a few of us, fellow students of Advaita, founded the ‚Vedanta Academy Germany' (VAG) with the blessings of my Master Raphael.

Raphael is a contemporary sage whose teaching is the inner unity of the Eastern and Western traditions. He is considered to be a ‚Jivanmukta', liberated while still alive, a Perfect Master. A few of us, a small group of close and intimate disciples, succeeded in bringing Him to Germany for a few seminars in the beginning of 2000. Meanwhile Raphael has reached a very advanced physical age and lives completely withdrawn in a hermitage in Italy. The name Raphael is a pseudonym and it represents both a state of consciousness and a special kind of Dharma. He is well known in the United States, India and in Europe as a Western Master in the One Tradition.
Elios received his name as a recommendation from Raphael. Raphael would never impose anything upon anyone.

Elios has taken on the task and the responsibility to teach the Unity of the Eastern and Western tradition in the German-speaking regions. The emphasis is on Advaita Vedanta and the work is thus physically grounded through the founding of the academy. Elios had already been asked by his Master to teach Advaita Vedanta a few years before this. For that purpose he had started a study group whose members later on became the founding members of the VAG.

Ever since we started working publicly people had asked more and more frequently for our own publications. It is true that I had been thinking of a book project for quite some time, but I had postponed it repeatedly, mainly because it is my nature to prefer to speak rather than to write. This was and is also true in the context of my scientific and therapeutic work. Then, a few years ago in a conversation with Raphael I mentioned almost resignedly, that Raphael had written so much himself on just about every topic regarding the Tradition that it wouldn‘t make much sense for me to also write something. Ultimately the answers to all possible questions could be found in his books. To that Raphael replied, as usual, briefly and precisely: Plato and Shankara have also written a lot. Does that mean that Raphael should not write anything? I remained silent with my mouth slightly agape: I had understood.

Another reason for my growing motivation to write had at least two more aspects. One is that Raphael‘s works are highly philosophical in the style of the great masters of the original texts. This is His Dharma here on earth and has to be carried out in that way. His works are highly sophisticated and are pure Advaita in accordance with the ancient Tradition. Thus the idea arose to perhaps write an Advaita book in a language that is easy to understand, without, however, distorting the greatness and the sublimity of the teaching. Not an easy endeavor.

In order to fulfill this requirement I have tried in the process to describe my own experiences from my childhood and youth with utmost honesty and clarity, so as to share them with the reader.

My pains and confusions are equally expressed here. Liberation is not possible without pain. Whoever wants to go to heaven must pass through hell first, according to many ancient scriptures. However, under the definition of hell falls also the prosperity-addicted behavior of western man, who believes he is able to live all his life in material abundance and indulge in emotionally-hedonistic happiness. This kind of attachment to the world is, strictly speaking, a state of hell because it prevents liberation.

Generally I made an effort to allow the pure essence of the teaching to resonate in all the chapters in spite of the more comprehensible language. The sensitive reader can soak it up between the lines or even perhaps contemplate it throughout several paragraphs, instead of just mentally absorbing the letters, words and sentences. In order not to neglect the main thread presented in the book's title it could not be helped but repeat to an extent some of the topic outlines and observe them from the ever-new perspectives of life practice.

As a classical Advaita teacher I cannot, I may not, and I do not desire to abandon the use of Sanskrit terms[1]. Sanskrit is the most ancient original language on earth. It is ascribed to Lord Brahma's consort, the goddess Saraswati. Each Sanskrit word carries great energy and embodies mantric powers. Some terms are very hard to translate without losing their potency. This becomes most obvious with the primordial sound OM or AUM. It cannot be translated into any language of the world. Likewise it cannot be decoded on the analytical and mental level. It can only be experienced, heard, seen or realized in a transcendentally altered state of consciousness. It defies any analysis or description. For it is far beyond any words.

---

1 For a better reading flow I have omitted the exact transliterated spelling in the main text; this can be found in the glossary.

Hence for me the essence of Advaita Vedanta was always the foundation upon which to build the themes and observations made within the framework of our present life experiences.

Another important reason for the creation of this book is the Neo-Advaita-scene. It makes the seeker believe that realization is a very simple thing, or even that it has already occurred and that we are not aware of it only because of our alienation, or what have you. This concept misleads some teachers to make fatal statements, which as a consequence rob us of any willpower or possibility of making our own decisions.

Still others claim that the refinement (they even say complexity) of the teachings of Shankara is totally superfluous. Then using this self-created axiom they pull out some supporting passages from the old teaching and then promise a considerable shortening of the "enlightenment process".

This would compare to somebody who is, let's say, on the Raja Yoga path of Patanjali and who follows his path of Ashtanga yoga, but picks out just two or three limbs of the eightfold path of yoga and declares everything else to be superfluous. This kind of thing simply doesn't work, it is not acceptable and it indicates that something very basic has not been understood. To illustrate it more graphically: when somebody has spent many months in darkness his eyes have to become accustomed to light very slowly. He cannot immediately look into the blazing sun. This is man's situation in the Dark Age: we can only approach the light of our souls, the light of God, step by step.

Aside from ONENESS God is also MULTIPLICITY. Brahman, who is One without a second, is the Whole. Saguna Brahman and Nirguna Brahman. The Upanishads say it with certainty: *All is truly Brahman!*

Basically, nobody is against such minimalist teachings. Because of the current zeitgeist they are well received by many people today. None of our impatient fellow citizens like making sustained effort. Fine, but then, please, don't classify these systems as Advaita Vedanta. In chapter 8 we will have a closer look at the differences between some of the Neo-aspects and classic Advaita.

In the process of writing, and while holding in mind the interested reader, I was concerned with creating a productive tension between spiritual curiosity and the thirst for knowledge on one hand, and on the other hand with reflections on my very personal confusions via recognition of mistakes, dead ends and omissions throughout my lifetime up to now – in my very own life task.

If at least one such spark has been triggered between the two poles of the rational and the spiritual then this book has fulfilled a useful purpose. Anything else lies with the discernment of the reader.

1. Advaita Vedanta in the 21st Century

With his commentary on the Mandukya Upanishad in the 8th Century AD in India, Gaudapada laid the foundation for the systematic completion of the Vedas. He and his principal disciple Govindapada tasked the still young Shankara with the work of producing a commentary on the Upanishads and the Brahmasutras. Because of his life's work he was regarded as Shankara-Acharya (acharya = teacher), he who codified Advaita into the form in which we know it today and which can be read in its transliterated Sanskrit entirety just as Shankaracharya wrote it.

One speaks of codification or of a codifier because Shankara summarized and systematized the essence of the ancient Vedas and the later Upanishads in an unprecedented and unsurpassed manner, thanks to his enlightened mind.

Today we live in the 21st Century of the Christian era. A brief review of the origins and roots of Advaita Vedanta will give us a better understanding of the history of this ancient teaching. Viewed from our current time Advaita Vedanta is the essence of the Upanishads, and the Upanishads in turn are the essence of the Vedas. The four Vedas have been recorded since 1500 BC. The relevant research is of the opinion that they've already existed in spoken form on this planet from about 6000 BC. There are Vedic texts in West India written in the form of the Sanskrit alphabet (Devanagari) from around 3000 BC.

Since its records began the essence of Advaita has been both partly hidden and partly available in the scriptures. Hence we can really speak of a 5,000-year-old literary tradition of Advaita Vedanta.

The time of the origin of the Upanishads, between1000-600 BC, in historical awareness is generally regarded as a time of spiritual awakening. The philosopher Karl Jaspers called this phenomenon an "Axial Age" because it marked a very significant transition: a transformation of the mind, a breakthrough into a new dimension - the questioning of human existence. Man, hitherto nature religious, began to build a new relationship with God. This period was initiated independently across various countries: Lao Tzu and Confucius in China, the Old Testament prophets in Israel, the Greek pre-Socratic philosophers and the Indian Rishis of the Upanishads. Plato in the West and Gautama Buddha in the East were the highlights of this beginning new era.

For the two and a half thousand years from the peak of the Axial Age, man has found himself on a journey of evolution of the mind. Upon closer inspection, it is more particularly a journey of the analytical mind (Vedanta: Manas) and less that of the soul. We owe all of our modern technological, social and cultural achievements to this new, burgeoning power of our mind. In just the last hundred years enormous progress has been made in the most impressive directions, as never before in history. But what of spiritual development, the serious religious questions about God, about realization?

With the training of the mind, that is, with the unfolding of the Logos (after Heraclitus and Plato, especially regarding the importance of the analytical, experiential mind), so-called empirical science gained the upper hand. It became all about proof, about the concrete, repeatable testing of facts, “facts”, which could optionally even be interpreted as laws. This is true not only for the highly acclaimed exact natural sciences, but also for the humanities and the economic and social sciences. Everything must be explainable and rationally comprehensible. Man wants to understand the world of names and forms completely. He wants to understand time and space and also intellectually approach the non-explainable – God.

Is God empirically verifiable or is HE or IT merely wishful thinking, passed down through generations and anchored in the collective consciousness? Vedanta says man of course has both the right and the ability to intellectually penetrate, analyze, explain this world of appearance and disappearance (Samsara), and finally to "subject" it to himself, as it says in the Bible. In the best case, this means to understand its laws and to live responsibly in and with them. In the worst, it means blind exploitation, limitless greed and ultimately destruction, whereby man himself saws off the branch on which he sits.

We will leave the current environmental debate aside here, a theme which clearly indicates a scenario of disaster, and state only: that man has badly abused his intellectual powers in many instances of his modern way of life and must now deal with the life-threatening consequences of his actions, and perhaps their possible containment.

In addition to the affirmation of the virtuous use of intellectual powers, above all the Vedanta emphasizes the recollection of what a person actually is: immortal Self! Empirical understanding stumbles over this, because it cannot deal with a non-finite state.

This does not fit any of its concepts. It simply cannot be, because everything is born, is present for a time, and goes again. Even large cycles, which from their scale may be considered endless, eventually pass away, and something new appears. In Samsara, the world of becoming, there is nothing, really nothing, which lasts. Everything is in a constant flux of change, even the seemingly fixed or constant. In the molecular field everything is constantly in motion. The mind knows this and therefore strictly rejects the notion that there is infinity or something absolute, timeless and limitless. It knows better. It observes and ultimately calculates very exactly with that most accurate of all the sciences, mathematics.

Modern man of the 21st Century was born into this mode of thought. As a child of his time, he believes in his senses, his mind, his feelings, his analytical thinking, he believes in his ability to accomplish, identifies himself with his body and thinks he is the doer, that he is the creator of the world, who knows his place in the solar system and will soon land on Mars. All this gives him the impression of greatness and grandeur, so he sees himself as the crown of creation, endowed with the privileges of the unconditional and almost divinely sanctioned use of resources: "subdue all upon the earth!"

Vedanta says: what a fatal misunderstanding! And immediately adds the explanation of why this is so. Since around about the Axial Age we live in what's called the Kali Yuga, following the Hindu concept of the World Ages, of which there are four in sequence. The Kali Yuga is known as the Dark Age, during which the ego comes to the fore, coupled with greed, anger, wrath, envy, destruction and forgetting of the Self, the soul. This is also called the "fall of the soul" in Advaita Vedanta. It has fallen from its divine origin, from the heights of the All-sublime, so to speak, fallen to the ground, and has almost been made helpless and overwhelmed by the forces of seduction, deception and projection (Maya) and materialism. For eons of incarnations, the nature of the human being has identified itself with the material aspect of the world that it has observed. So it came to the fateful conclusion: the body, that's me, that's what I am.

But, thank God, there are the old traditions. They remind us again and again, in every age, and gently, of our origin. They encourage the Manas towards the known questions: Where am I, where am I going, what is my destiny, do I have free will, etc.?

Advaita Vedanta is one such old tradition. Strictly speaking, there really is only One Tradition, one that presents itself differently depending on the zeitgeist of the era. Its essence, however, is immutable. This is so because it is not of human origin. In the true and proper sense it is revelation, in whatever form of communication it presents itself: written, oral, by a means of miracle, in the form of a master/teacher or in silence. It is always present whether noticed or unnoticed by people, it is pure wisdom, truth, transcending the world, beyond space and time, unaffected by all impermanence, and it taps gently on the shoulder of a man who has attained maturity. It finds him, he doesn't find it.

In the Western world we see many societies and nations threatened by complete burnout. People live in a strong field of tension between labor-economy and personal growth-spirituality. Work serves several purposes simultaneously: the search for meaning, psychological self-actualization, self-preservation, livelihood protection, social integration, sense of belonging, recognition, appreciation, and so on. These are complex life constellations, in which formal, temporal, social, emotional, future and current problem areas overlap, calling for strong internal and external coping strategies, differentiated discernment and a high degree of clarity.

Are we as modern people already so resistant to stress that we can withstand all of this? Our full hospitals and outpatient treatment centers, such as physician's and psychologist's practices, speak for themselves: no, we're not able to cope with it. This means that man, thanks to his highly developed mental abilities, has created living conditions that easily overwhelm him psychosomatically. The rate of evolution of the mind is a good deal faster than that of the body and the emotions. The latter two are lagging behind considerably. And this significantly erodes one's health.

Do we have any way out of this situation – or even any corrective steps we can take? We do posses a complex medical and psychological technology, which reacts to this situation and tries to move the ailing individual back to more stability. But what can we do? How can we create a new stability in our lives, one which transcends the wide range of tasks demanded in the workplace, in the family and in society, a stability that goes beyond merely regenerative relaxation?

The answer is found in true, sincere spirituality. True and earnest effort must be unconditional if the seeker wants to achieve progress. Half-hearted intellectual toying with a spiritual path, occasional exercises or even participating in practices just to fit in, not only contribute nothing, but can actively foster a person's vanity, which in turn can lead to disturbing results.

A path like the classic Advaita Vedanta of Shankaracharya calls forth the whole essence of a man in a holistic manner. The initial impression that this is an easily understood path evaporates rapidly when one understands – or even feels – what a proper piece of work it is to build the necessary qualifications[2], without which one makes absolutely no progress. However, this should not discourage anyone from actively engaging with the Sacred Tradition. Quite the contrary. Whoever feels the urge for liberation within, feels all the more called to make friends with this highly

2 Higher discrimination, letting go of all attachments, unquenchable thirst for freedom, mental stillness, etc. More about qualifications in later chapters.

refined spiritual path, and to ever more thoroughly investigate who and what this "I" is.

Another question arises in today's life practice: how can one integrate an ancient Wisdom Teaching into modern everyday life and its current events? Do we still understand this ancient teaching today, is it still up to date or is it more suited to spiritual romantics? The Teaching has been present throughout all the ages. Every age wonders this question alike and all too easily considers religion, philosophies or mystical teachings outdated and obsolete. Interestingly, however, only for as long as a society is doing well. In good times society quickly becomes arrogant and with dizzying ease falls for superficial materialism, idealism, or any kind of seductive ideology. Raphael calls this attitude "psychological comfort rather than true and genuine spirituality."

The main problem that prevents us from embarking on an authentic spiritual path intensively and with full responsibility, with total and loving dedication, lies in one particular aspect of man. It is his ego, the little self. Vedanta provides us with the exact structure of the framework of the human being[3] with unrivalled clarity. Here it should suffice to say that it is the Ahamkara, the I-sense, the ego, that which collaborates in close liaison with the mind (Manas). This is a psychic organizational structure grown over thousands of existences, one that seems unshakeable and unavoidable. It is part of our inner organs[4]. No one can easily escape the influence of these innermost components of our being. After all, these forces work with different states of consciousness, such as the unconscious, the subconscious and the sleeping and waking consciousness. But in deep sleep, this sense complex is totally switched off, as it also is in the so-called fourth state of consciousness, the superconscious.

3 see graphic ibid. page 124-125

4 Antahkarana, the internal operating structure, which we in modern psychology call psyche. A very complex mental-emotional structure. See graphic page 126

Shankara says that even experienced or great yogis, even if they have control over many Siddhi powers[5]5, will shy away from facing this very special step, absolutely necessary for Liberation: the abandonment of the ego, the death of the ego. Advaita calls it the initiatory death of the philosopher.

Without the death of the little self, without the abandonment of thinking and without detachment from all desires and worldly attachments, liberation, salvation or enlightenment remain simply concepts of Manas, and thus ultimately useless in the course of spiritual effort.

On one hand, the present time in the middle of the Kali Yuga provides us with considerable resistance to a spiritual breakthrough into the Universal. On the other hand, it also serves as a powerful stimulus to the development of a new and fruitful polarity within the world of creation and the universe. It provides the opportunity for absolute detachment from all sense impressions, for the return to the Self, for the liberation from the yoke of the ego and all illusion.

According to Vedanta, man lives in the world for only one purpose: to break free from the delusions, projections and illusions of empirical world appearances both internally and externally. This underlying, hidden power is, according to tradition, Maya, the creative principle, that diverse, fascinating, but nonetheless misleading appearance, the primal illusion or the unreal, non-being. Although this immense deception constitutes a formidable barrier on the road to liberation, Maya is divine, it is an expression of the almighty power of God (Isvara) and therefore also Reality. The universe and the creation of all levels and worlds are, from the standpoint of the Absolute (Brahman), only an appearance on the divine canvas, but they have, as Raphael puts it, a degree of reality. So the classic

5 Supernatural powers such as clairvoyance, psychokinesis, levitation, etc

Vedantin doesn't reject the world or the body as mere illusion, but assigns a degree of truth to it. The formula is then as follows:

> Maya is illusion, Maya is divine,
> So the Divine also implies
> that illusion, that everything, is God.
> or:
> Reality is Divine Presence,
> Deception is multiplicity.

In the current Dark Age the power of deception and the almost unshakable belief in matter, energy and body is extremely strong. Thus, it may be regarded as a blessing to have the opportunity to break out of the cage of captivity of Ego-Manas with the help of a true Teaching and a true Teacher/Master. But not everyone is ready, willing or able.

Nowadays many busy themselves with spiritual teachings and in running from teacher to teacher, but few work persistently on the dissolution of the egoic encrustations of the psycho-mental apparatus. Granted, there are some things you can pursue yourself, self-taught and alone, but for many it takes a teacher whose mere presence is already a blessing, and a kind of initiation. Pure-in-Heart spirituality is not a simple wellness program to make your body and mind feel good; on the contrary, it is genuinely hard work to understand the hidden lower being and to gradually overcome it.

In the process of giving up individuality we begin to blink in the dazzling light of Universality – the full view of the interwoven Whole, One View – instead of separation and multiplicity.

2. Desire for Liberation, but no Time

Appearance of light

As a young boy of preschool age in the middle of the 20th Century, one winter I found myself in a warm living room heated by a coal stove, and looking at the window. Frost patterns in beautiful shapes glinted from bottom to top up the windowpane. In those days this was a normal appearance with the simple, thin panes of glass that were then used. It was still light outside, when I suddenly saw a strange light, a spherical, blinding, bright light phenomenon that danced on the outside in flowing movements up and down the windowpane, as if it wanted to slide into the parlor. After a few minutes it disappeared again. My parents didn't notice it and when I remarked on it, suggested it had probably been car headlights. But it was still light enough outside that a headlight could hardly have produced this effect, and then as well this phenomenon appeared as a sphere, not as a simple light projection. Three-dimensional holographic laser technology was still far in the future. So what was it?

Many years later I recalled this event that had so much impressed me at the time, and interpreted it as an announcement of a luminous future: imminent encounters with the Divine light, the radiating of the soul force, both as an inner and outer light that can reveal the finer senses. In retrospect, this interpretation has proven itself quite viable, because there has always been a very subtle, but clearly effective force in my life that has not only supported me in bad times, but which has increasingly proved itself to be a core, basic element in my life. A force that has never left me since.

My early experience says something about the initial spark that happens in our hearts. This spark is a call for a change in direction in life, turning to the Holy Divine or turning away from the profane-material. In the Western world today these different groups can be found:

1. **People in whom the divine slumbers.**

   They live a life of materialism, preferably in prosperity and luxury. They aim at psycho-material worldly happiness in terms of occupation, career, marriage, children, friends, home and possessions. Their attitude to life ranges from atheistic-materialistic to nihilistic. For them, with death the individual being ceases to exist. Brain death means darkness, without consciousness, without perception, dissolution of all subjectivity, the end of everything.

2. **Pious and religious people.**

   This group is either inclined to varying degrees of religiousness, or due to their upbringing they are pious, devoted servants of the Lord, according to Christian teaching. Piety develops as a strong emotion, either in childhood already or through the most violent and traumatic life events. Religiousness, however, can also arise on a purely rational level via study or due to situational interests, with little emotional overlay. In both cases, the sense of a divine existence may flare up and bring about a turning point in life. The feeling of inner guidance perhaps springs up in them.

3. **People with a clear spiritual orientation**

   These are mostly souls who, thanks to their personal karma during this existence, quite naturally feel the inner impulse to start the way back to the original source of their beginnings. If this impulse is strong, they will intensively search for knowledge and experience. Perhaps – and this is probable – they come into contact with advanced souls, teachers or masters. They are genuine, interested individuals, seekers or aspirants with or without a traditional path.

4. **Experienced and Great Souls**

   After many existences, two possibilities arise. Either the final journey of life begins, one that carries within itself a high chance for the last kick to no-return. Or, a being already realized returns to this world of becoming to help those fallen in ignorance, and who will return to Mahasamadhi[6] after termination of this Dharma.

Only this last, the fourth group, requires either little or no help on the spiritual path. The first three groups are characterized by a strong sense of ego in conjunction with a mind that is colored due to individual tendencies and qualities. The psychological structures are often hardened in such a way that in the present existence a spiritual drive is out of the question. Nonetheless, any kind of spiritual encounter or discussion will leave an impression in the unconscious psyche, reappearing at some point, perhaps in a much later existence and eventually yielding results.

---

6 Mahasamadhi, the great and final Samadhi, in which a realized being willfully plunges to leave behind forever all bodily limitations (Upadhis). There is no death in the traditional sense, but pure transcendence, switching into the Brahman-state, the Absolute as Satchidananda.

Except for the fourth group all complain of a chronic lack of time, which prevents them from dealing seriously and permanently with spiritual questions. The impulse is quite real, but there is a lack of opportunity to effectively come to rest. The everyday life of family, career, work and livelihood takes its toll. This manifests as a plethora of thoughts, a never-ending stream of thoughts, as a taxing upsurge of emotional experiences, as anxiety, stress, frenzy, distraction, lack of concentration, all the way up to complete burnout. This raises a serious question: how can there be room for spirituality in such an all-engrossing modern life?

Along with this come some other general facts of human life, which act to restrict an active spiritual life. We sleep almost half of our lives away. We spend a lot of time mentally or physically ill and suffering, with the family and with leisure activities, we busy ourselves intensively with food and drink, with shopping and cooking and housework. A lot of time is just wasted, and we are bored (Tamas Guna) or hyperactive (Rajas Guna). All of these are severe delays on the spiritual path. Even in retirement, some end up living a very hectic life. They take care of the grandchildren, renovate the house, pursue hobbies, are active in associations, travel, etc., to demonstrate that they still have a meaningful life, or, as they say, simply to enjoy life.

Here one does not question or doubt the need of the individual for a wellness program for body and mind. It is nonetheless surprising that the members of the first two or three groups, both during their working life and in retirement age, hardly ever find their way to themselves.

From the beginning of its appearance on this planet the Vedantic tradition knew that this is a very serious problem, and is particularly evident in an age like the present. The Kali Yuga is considered a time when the ego prevails in its ignorance and is totally caught up in worldly needs and comforts, desires, instincts and senses. The Kama-Manas (psychological pleasure-pain center) regulates these inclinations. Since for the bulk of humanity life is primarily about living out driven and sensory-controlled impulses, and given the huge range of time-intensive activities, there is virtually nothing left over for serious spiritual efforts. So when or how can modern man do anything at all for this salvation of soul so frequently referred to?

We will now investigate some basic instructions and methods for the control of psychic powers, about which great teachers such as Sivananda, Krishnananda, Vivekananda, Sri Yukteswar and Raphael all in principle agree. Their application follows natural laws that help the individual very quickly and effectively attain a higher level of self-control, rather than freeze in the mind-set of a helpless victim.

When Advaita Vedantins speak of mind they mean the complex inner organ that is called in classical terminology Antahkarana[7], or sometimes fourfold mind. It exists as

- understanding mind (Manas)
- Connection with the higher intellect (Buddhi)
- ego / I-sense (Ahamkara)
- subconscious (Citta)

The lower nature of man must be overcome by pursuing the goal of liberation. One of the main problems is the focus on the physical body. Thanks not least to the manipulative advertising of the mass media, one wants the body to be clean, healthy, strong, beautiful and productive. It is crammed with abundant over-nutritious food, preened, groomed, perfumed, and trained with sports. If it is sick, it is supplied with medicine, it is operated upon and rehabilitated.

---

7 see page 126

The body is a key instrument in the competition of comparison in both sexes. Its sexual and physical power are considered top criteria for attractiveness, reproduction, and even viewed as an expression of the soul. The body as a temple of God (Biblical statement) must be cherished and cared for. This is the top priority for most people.

There's no doubt that as a means of interacting with the physical world the body is important and necessary. But is the amount of time we devote to it reasonable in view of the true calling of human beings? Your purpose is liberation and your task is to develop the higher nature at cost of the lower. Thus teach the Upanishads. Who devotes the mind at least the same or even greater time than the body these days? It seems we are still far from understanding what Goethe, in acknowledgement of the Upanishads, once expressed: the body follows the mind and not vice-versa.

And how can it really make sense, that one is primarily concerned with the effect rather than the cause? Still today, for example, the focus of most orthodox scientific medicine falls for this inverse relationship, groping around blindly in the dark. They consider the mind to be a simple secretion of the brain, like bile from the liver. With the refusal of the brain to work (usually referred to as death) the mind therefore vanishes. There's no more active organ and no secretion, so no more mind. That sounds very logical - but it is simply wrong, and a fatal conclusion for a seeker believing in science. These days especially there are so many reports of near-death experiences and astral travel in the subtle light body, that this absurdly outdated thesis cannot possibly be maintained any longer.

Whoever has experienced just once, even if only for a brief moment, that the mind is not bound to the body, is freed forever from this delusional paradigm of medical science. So let us all, in compassion and responsibility, call out to all who wish to seriously work on themselves:

> From this moment onward concern yourself more with the mind than with the body. Learn exactly the nature and the methods of operation of the mind and begin life in a completely new modality. Whoever controls the mind, controls not only the body and the emotions, but opens a gateway to higher spirituality, for entry into the Universal.

The mind-thought process is based on an infinite chain reaction of ideas with and without sense impressions. It immediately takes the form of the object of thought. For example, in summer we might think of a delicious ice-cream. The result is a strong desire to taste it. A gradual thought sequence sets in, from the path to the ice-cream shop, to choosing the ice-cream, to contact with the sales person, to the payment, to the enjoyment of the dessert and the anticipation of the associated pleasant feelings. Thus one thought follows the other, amounting to thousands of them. In this way man is being driven automatically, largely an unconscious victim of his automatic mind-world, which is primarily designed for more or less important gratifications. The mind is not only the sixth sense, as Krishna says in the Bhagavad Gita, but it is also independent of the senses. It can bring forth all the sense forces from itself and present them as life experience to the consciousness in the waking as well as in the dream state.

Maybe it will motivate us to allow more time for the mind when we hear of yet another relevant point from the Tradition. It is one of the most essential points of all on the path from birth, life, and aging to death. It relates to the very last thought in the death process. Shankara and Krishna, in texts such as the Vivecacudamani and the Bhagavad Gita, point to the vast and powerful force and meaning that the last thought in life has on future lives on this planet. We ask ourselves: is it possible to control that? The germination and growing power of the last thought basically follows a simple mechanism. Everyone has by their very nature certain tendencies and desires, that they look to fulfill over a lifetime. Longings and hopes spring from the power of their minds, from their thoughts, feelings, and imagination. This conglomeration of tastes, temperaments, attitudes and values, applied over a lifetime, leaves different degrees of thought impressions (Sanskrit: Sankalpa). At the hour of death all these impressions arise from the subconscious, from the hard drive of the mind so to speak, one after the other in a hierarchic order. They say one sees the movie of one's life play out in the mind's eye. But it is not only chronologically arranged scenes that one sees, but also memories of spatiotemporal quality of experiences with all the stored sense-impressions. The course unfolds more according to the priorities that we once assigned to the events, persons or wishes. The Vedas and the Upanishads refer emphatically to those circumstances at the hour of death, because it is at this narrow point in the course of a life that it will be exactly determined how and in what form things will proceed for this entity. In the ancient wisdom legends of the Puranas an account is given of a man who has lived a righteous and spiritual life. At his hour of death his fear of snakes awakens involuntarily and unconsciously - and thus in his next life he becomes a snake. So, according to this law, everyone becomes that with which he is identified most often and with greatest emotional intensity. He then takes the form of that which has most strongly bound or captured him. This is not a disaster in itself, because every life has its own particular experience, but for those who strive for liberation it is far from the most advantageous pathway.

Blessed is the being, then, that through constant and sincere quest for truth, for God and enlightenment, thinks of Atman in the last seconds of his life. What a gift to receive this due to the fruits of thought and actions – whether over a lifetime or for a long time! Sivananda calls to us in his writings, here somewhat paraphrased:

> Think always of the immortal Self during your lifetime, then in the hour of death there arises naturally the Atman-Thought.
>
> This thought will without doubt set you free from the endless chain of birth and death, and lead you to immortality, and you will attain eternal bliss. This man either goes into the Universal World, or even attains the last liberation of Nirvikalpa as Satchitananda.

Our mind is often compared to a mirror that can reflect truth and reality. If it is dull and dirty, one only sees the sense world of Samsara, and takes this for reality, and in so doing conditions the subconscious. Through cleaning, examination and distancing, the mirror of the mind becomes ever more clear and increasingly reflects the Only Reality. The cleaning procedure needs these components, for example, which should become a life practice:

- Anxiety-free and systematic practice of spiritual exercises (Sadhana)
- Proven and suitable Meditation practice
- Devotion and profound love for the Divine (Bhakti)
- Karma Yogic practice in the form of selfless work without thought of profit and personal benefit of any kind (altruistic orientation)
- Wisdom as a result of razor sharp higher discrimination (Buddhi-Viveka)
- The constant question "Who am I?", as Ramana Maharshi has recommended (Vichara)
- Repetition of the name of God or one of the names of God as a Mantra, and the flooding of consciousness with it (Japa)

- Study of the sacred writings of a tradition, which has manifested itself in different times in different cultures, such as Gnosticism, Kabbalah, Orphism, or Vedanta. Of these, Vedanta has the clearest articulation and the greatest depth.
- Find a community where one can study and practice with spiritually like-minded people under the guidance of a qualified teacher / guru (Satsanga)
- Well-balanced, sattvic food filled with light energy and vital vibration
- Depending on the individual and his naturally conditioned need for mind-body interaction, practice aspects/exercises of the eightfold path of yoga (Raja Yoga-Ashtanga Yoga) according to the sage Patanjali Maharshi.

Whoever adheres to these guidelines and practices them diligently in his life will attain liberation, perhaps even while still alive. That sounds all-consuming and complex, but is no more complex than the usual modern welter of mundane activities, all of which ultimately lead to the misery of worldly suffering and an uncertain rebirth.

What the uncontrolled mind can bring about in the life of a man who has no time for his qualifications, doctors, lawyers, educators, theologians, social workers and psychologists can sing a song of woe about. Diseases, and especially psychosomatic suffering[8], fill the waiting rooms of doctors and lengthen the waiting lists of psychotherapists. We get older, but not necessarily wiser, as some presumptuous, or perhaps just naïve, people believe. We are also not getting any healthier, because these days diseases that usually occur in old age are appearing much earlier, such as forms of dementia, Alzheimer's, diabetes, osteoporosis, arthritis, blood

8 This term shows very nicely and precisely that the mind acts in two ways; on the body (Soma) and on itself (Psyche).

cancer, age-related eye disorders, motor disorders, premature wear and tear, fatigue etc.

For advanced aspirants of truth, it is a kind of sacred duty to provide assistance to all who have gone astray, or have come to a dead-end. Vedanta may provide assistance for all their supposed time problems in a natural and systematic way, with the help of a suitable teacher. Help to those who live in our own time, our contemporaries in general and especially those among them who believe that they have no time for the single most important life-mission of achieving liberation.

The secular mind is poisoned. The purified mind must be enriched with thoughts of God, Isvara or Brahman. God's presence needs to be felt, His all-pervading strength to be sensed. In this way, over the course of many lives the wrongly conditioned mind is gradually anchored in divine consciousness. Luther's principle of "sola fide" ("by faith alone") applies mainly to the qualified among men who submit themselves to new, sacred rules. Then the grace of God will raise men back even to the Godhead. The path leads from duality to unity.

There exists in the entire Universe

No greater, more meaningful event.

Shanti!

3. Where do I Stand – Where do I Go?

Experience the All

One day, during my third or fourth school year, I was alone at home, as so often happened. Father and mother were at work. In the middle of the week it was quiet in our urban multi-family house. I sat on the sofa and began, quite abruptly and to my own astonishment, to ponder the vastness of the universe. This was at a time when no documentaries on astronomical topics were being broadcast in the media – and anyway at that time we only had a radio. Nor, at that age, had we heard of anything like that in school. So there was no cause to be thinking about the universe, of all things, from outside influences. At that tender age I simply lacked the intellectual maturity for such a complex subject. So from where did the impetus come for this very particular inapposite experience? It could only have come from within. But of course at that moment I wasn't thinking about all of that, I wasn't capable of such reflections - the event just happened.

I sat quietly, lost in thought on the familiar sofa. Above me, sitting on a long shelf, were all my favorite stuffed animals that had always comforted me so wonderfully, even when I was sick. My mind floated upward to the stars.

I felt the ungraspable vastness of space. There were no sensory impressions other than distance in the infinite space of the universe. The rest of the world disappeared around me, I felt neither heat nor cold, nor sound. There was nothing in my mind or senses apart from the experience of this infinite expansion. It was overwhelming. Then suddenly I had the feeling that I would go crazy, would lose my mind, that I had to surrender, and would lose control over the body or the mind. I panicked, became extremely unsettled and full of fear – and then I just sat back on the couch. I simply could not believe, much less explain, what had just happened here.

When, many years ago, I once told my master of this event, he said with a smile: "Oh what a shame, you could have learned to fly at such a young age." With 'flying' he meant the liberation of the soul from the body, or more precisely, the detachment of the subtle body from the physical body or the immediate translocation to another place in space and in a different time. "Then you would have been able to circumnavigate the entire Milky Way in one second," he added in a more serious tone.

At the time of this miraculous event, I had no idea of where on the ladder of spiritual development I was as a human being, let alone where I would go. Such essential and philosophical questions were reserved for later in life.

These days one often hears and reads the term "self-actualization". In most cases, this term is used as one of psychological significance: as a synonym for a particular life plan for all that one wants to achieve in this life. These include such things as family, friends, career, hobbies, travel, culture, health, and most certainly, just wanting to have fun. For decades trade and industry have actively sought not only to support all these life pleasures, but to awaken more and more desires and wants for things that man really doesn't need, and to anchor them in the subconscious by long-lasting media suggestion.

It's almost tragic what modern man, without using his own discrimination, feeds and allows to be fed to his subconscious. Most do not realize that this content influences their lives and, strictly speaking, also their deaths. This is because the content and priorities of the subconscious determine the next birth, as we have discussed in the previous chapter. But an even greater tragedy is that the average person – which means most people – considers himself to be small and insignificant. And when he hears of astrophysics and fantastic computer animations or sees images from the Hubble telescope, then it becomes really clear how tiny he is and how unspectacularly he floats through the universe on this big planet. He feels how little influence he has on anything, merely a plaything of nature. In hopeless helplessness, with a sense of powerlessness against the overwhelming forces of nature and the incomprehensible grandeur of the universe, many push aside these large-scale relationships to physics and plunge into the familiar hustle and bustle of their everyday lives. Here, in practical life, one can at least have an occasional uplifting sense of achievement. But one also experiences a huge amount of suffering here. This is shown by suicide and accident rates, separation and divorce data, and widespread illness, depression and anxiety. No one can be sure of a life of health and happiness, of prosperity and peace. Terrorism, war, hatred, anger, bloody revolutions and misanthropy raise their fearsome faces in this Dark Age. So what's the point of driving blindly and naively through this short, precious lifetime? In any case it certainly doesn't help to achieve spiritual realization, and not even to achieve psychological self-actualization.

Man must urgently become aware of his real size and strength again. But in an ego-less manner, or otherwise megalomania, abuse of power and ruthlessness immediately take over rule.

> "It is the greatest sin to think that you are weak. None is greater; know that you are Brahman ... No action can give you freedom; only knowledge[9] can give it"[10]
>
> *Vivekananda.*

The lower nature of man must be exposed and overcome in order to give his higher nature some free space to develop. The ego and mind are, thanks to the way they support each other, instruments of a prison that make us believe that this dungeon is normal, that it is our nature. But, as in the parable of the cave of the divine Plato, the same fatal error happens here, that of identifying with the mere shadows of existence, being shut up in the body. In this way we become disabled people who must live, act and think in bondage. The identification with the shadow causes countless rebirths, in the manner of a vicious circle. We think we are living, but compared to the infinite possibilities of our divine origin, it is just a kind of vegetating away from life to life. Whether this vegetating happens with or without luxury plays a very secondary role. Forgetting our selves is so strongly and deeply rooted in the subconscious depths that without an additional impulse from karmic merits or by the grace of an authentic teacher no light at the end of the tunnel of existence is seen for an endlessly long time.

In meditation, in contemplation, when studying the scriptures or in Satsang, we learn where we are on the scale of spiritual development, step by step, and we also perceive an ever more illuminated impression of where the soul's journey goes. Shankara gives us an important clue for spiritual self-discovery. He says awareness (in the sense of pure awareness) is the last proof of Beingness. This awareness is self-luminous and self-aware. It is independent of the

---

9 What is meant is Jnana, immediate vision and knowledge of the Self beyond the individual and the ego.

10 Vivekananda: Gespraeche auf den tausend Inseln, (Conversations on the Thousand Islands), Geneva, 1944 p.140f

senses and all the tools of the lower nature of man. It is without cause, without qualities, without any conditions, eternally free.

This awareness is the higher nature of the human being. It is Atman-Brahman, the eternal witness, the Absolute. A major difficulty is that we are in the world of the relative, characterized by the duality of subject and object. Consequently for the less developed human being there arises a permanent separation between subject and object in his view of life, between mine and thine, life and death, between God and man. This gap seems unbridgeable as long as the separation is maintained. And the separation remains as long as, in sweet harmony, Manas and ego create individuality with all its needs. It is a cycle, which the Buddha once recognized and described as the Wheel of 84, an almost endlessly long cycle of birth, life, joy, suffering, death and rebirth.

The serious seeker stands before a very big problem: the Manas cannot grasp the Absolute, has no clue about it, because the Absolute by far exceeds its nature. Even and especially, language is not sufficient to express the Absolute. Vivekananda puts it this way:

> "Prakriti is the nature of the world and is subject to change. Changeable thoughts expressed in changeable words can never prove the Absolute. We achieve [in the best case, E.] a standardization of the word, the highest abstraction, but not the removal of the relative."[11]

To the question, "Where am I in life?", someone perhaps replies I am a father, mother, lawyer, painter, office worker, unemployed, rich, alive and well, scattered in the middle of an important project, or I am a seeker of truth. Such a question seems quite normal, if not actually banal. But not when you assign a new dimension to it. Then it becomes an analysis of my ability, which I have thus

---

11 Vivekananda , ibid., Page 142

far developed, to recognize my nature and depth, to reflect on the meaning of my life and to know my position on the question of God and the possibility of life after my time on earth. But it doesn't help to do this as if you were just filling out a checklist on a psychological test. You can't mentally figure out where you are spiritually, you can only feel it. With the onset of serious search the seeker experiences an inner change through his Sadhana (practice) and the contact with his teacher, and this change can sometimes set in slowly and sometimes quickly. At first, it is only a sense of change in the thinking-feeling-behavior. Then actual changes, also observable by others, enter the picture, changes that you would not normally have associated with or predicted for this person. The person touched by spiritual fire begins with the development of qualifications[12] for a life in freedom, a life without fear. Regardless of social, economic, cultural or political modalities, the spiritual asceticism of an aspiring Jnana Yogi or Advaitin begins to take effect. In the most favorable scenario, Sadhana can be built up to a 24 hour practice, which includes the dream state. But this takes a lot of concentration, patience, perseverance, conviction, will and intuition. If it were as easy as some Neo-Advaitins swear it is, then the world would soon be swamped by enlightened beings.

Now we come to the second part of our initial question: Where am I going? Classical Advaita Vedanta has a prompt and very concise answer:

> You're not going anywhere. You are already here. Because you are. You've always been here, never actually gone anywhere. You are the timeless, eternal Self, Atman. It's you, Tat Tvam Asi. You have just forgotten.

That sounds very instructive, meaningful, incredible and far-reaching, but can mere mortals really do something with it? Probably not.

---

12 According to Vedanta anything that can dissolve the ego-Manas complex.

Granted, the Vedantin speaks to his students and those interested in this way, because verbally it comes very close to the Truth and is philosophically consistent. But to effectively reach those people less prepared – those in the relative, who perceive everyday life as the sole true reality, the usual physical and intellectual environment with all its worries, problems and crises - such a proposition is not sufficient.

This advice is considerably more practical: until now you've gone into the outer world, searched for happiness there, in pleasures, in the satisfaction of intense desires and needs, and perhaps even in good, positive feelings. You still need to go inside, deep inside, deeper than the feelings, finer than any feeling that you've had so far. Far past your mind, beyond the I and you, beyond the I-sense, in a dimension far past all experiences of life known to date, to transcend all the known and trusted and solidly anchor yourself in being.

You ask what needs to be done, quite specifically, what do you have to do? Here again you run astray with the mind and its empirical limitations. Open your heart, your spiritual heart, the Heart Chakra (Anahata). You can activate it through the breath, through a Mantra and the required concentration. The Heart (not the physical organ!) is the key to transcendence and overcoming the Ego-Manas alliance. When it is sufficiently wide open Universal energy flows and the being enters a world of splendor and light. This is the beginning of your true survival and the end of the classic struggle for survival. From now on many things happen as if by themselves. Your meditation deepens, and maybe you reach Samadhi. Your entire being, previously known in the form of your personality, turns itself inside out, taking on an altruistic rather than self-centered tenor. You have only one desire: to reach God, to become God, to be God once again – your natural state, your birthright. From now on you will be a blessing to all people, whether you teach in public or spend the rest of your days on earth in silence. Your presence alone is a blessing.

For a being with activated Heart Energy there is no longer the question "Where am I going?", dominated by life's attendant problems and the uncertainty of a life after death. The Universally revitalized man has overcome the Ego-Manas-forces and even death. At the hour of his transition, he remains fully conscious and aware of what is happening. In his own lifetime he has overcome the primal fear of man, the fear of death. He has proven once and for all the independence of his existence. Without the slightest conceptualized thought he knows something with utter certainty:

> I am not the body, I am not the mind, not the feelings, I'm not all of that which I previously thought I was. I am free, I am beyond all bondage. I AM is the only thing that is true, without illusion, without deception, free of any projection.

Having established my position in the hierarchy of being reasonably successfully, and the question of my further evolution is sufficiently clear, I am now highly motivated to begin and not to postpone any further. Life is much too short to neglect even one day of spiritual work, of the way home, the path of no return, the way to eternal bliss. Once we have clearly recognized our true mission, then there actually is no way back. From a certain degree of realization onwards the way ahead is straight. It's true that we continue living in this world and carrying out our obligations, but the world has nothing more to offer us for our salvation. All things transitory and fleeting (the world of becoming, Samsara) slip way down on the priority list of existence. The new values are freedom, detachment, independence, lack of desire, fearlessness, giving instead of taking, intuitive knowledge and an unspeakable joy beyond sensory stimuli.

When does the reader of these lines begin with this new life? It is a renewal, a kind of baptism and rebirth while still alive. "Anyone who wants to enter into the kingdom of heaven, must first be born again", said Christ. This rebirth began with baptism as a symbolic act. Every encounter (Darshan) with a great spiritual teacher is an initiation that brings something into movement inside. It opens doors and floods the being with Universal divine love. This can be the start of a second, new life. The past no longer counts, the future is now shaped in the name of God (Bhakti, Karma Yoga) by abdication from being the doer. There is no more worrying about the future. Only the present counts, only this moment in being, a moment of eternity, its sweet foretaste.

O Ishvara,
may Blessings be!

4. Dealing with Pain – Separation, Death, Grief

Father calls

In the 1980s I lived with my young family in Bavaria on a lake called Chiemsee. My father died during this time. Many months before his death I was twice called to his bedside, within a few weeks of each other, by my mother and the family doctor because each time it appeared that he was dying. Ignoring the 700 kilometer distance, I drove in haste to my parent's house each time. And both times something happened that seemed miraculous. Each time father was in a coma-like state in his bed at home. I stood at the foot of the bed and gazed with compassion at him. After a few minutes he opened his eyes and became conscious, and was immediately attended to. My father loved his son above all else. There was a deep and strong inner relationship of fatherly love with me. It was most likely this inner bond, this particularly powerful energy that twice brought him back to life. I used no methodology or technique, I was just present with a loving heart. Even a year after his death, I felt the presence of my father at Chiemsee.

Time and distance are irrelevant in such matters. Thereafter I celebrated a blessing ritual for him that was meant to help free his soul, which was still bound to the world. After that I had no more experiences of his presence again. He could now begin a new life cycle in the subtle levels of the Taijasa[13].

In this way I was able to learn with what immense power the SPIRIT is with us when we open our hearts to divine love. Divine, impersonal love and human-emotional love naturally merge when they meet, like two drops of water into a larger one.

• • •

It's hard to judge what kind of pain a person finds more severe, more intense and more threatening - the physical-neural, the emotional, or the spiritual. Does the last even exist at all? How does the advanced student deal with pain? Does his coping strategy differ from that of people from the normal social context?

The fact is that every person, regardless of his degree of development, is confronted with painful events in his life.

Here is a brief story recorded by an affected person:

May: demented mother suffers a stroke. Because the home care service present responds immediately she is very quickly attended to by a doctor. The physiological and neural damage remains limited. Dementia, however, has progressed much further. This means that the mother is even less approachable, can communicate even less, is even more depersonalized; she finds it even harder to remember something, to recognize people and assign them a name. During the next few months, she is tied to the bed and the wheelchair, needs catheters and diapers, is incapable of feeding herself. Rehabilitation efforts, staying in intensive care units for acute cases alternates with short-term

13 A subtle, light-filled plane of existence, where most of the deceased arrive.

care in two-to-three-week rotations. Then the terminus: the nursing home. The apartment, thus far retained, must now be given up. The family had wanted to accept an admission to a nursing home only when there was no other choice. With the disposal of parent's furniture and the many memorabilia from childhood and adolescence there begins a gradual material and emotional letting-go process for the persons concerned. Is this a forthcoming end to a family history? The mother is the last survivor of the parents. Yet she still lives.

December: Sunday evening. The nursing home calls, the mother has taken a turn for the worse. Half a night spent on Mother's bed presents the image of a dying woman, a struggle with death in full swing, facial features stamped with suffering and all the many accompanying side effects of great emotional pain. It is felt that she has already arrived on the other side. Then suddenly comes normal, peaceful sleep. Calm spreads over the being. The facial expression becomes relaxed. In the following week a continuous overall improvement takes place with gains in strength, and a smile appears on her face.

Another visit to the mother on Friday afternoon. She recognizes her son, she smiles constantly, she wants to cuddle, wants closeness, lots of closeness, more and more, there are lots of hugs, head to head, forehead to forehead, without end. She is reasonably responsive, understands without being able to respond. It can be seen from the expression on her face. Wonderful development this week. Contented, grateful ride home.

Saturday Afternoon: During a call with a friend, the call-waiting tone sounds on the phone. The nursing home. It reports quite succinctly about the mother's sudden and unexpected death. - On the bed of the mother. Her hands are warm, facial features peaceful. Spiritual accompaniment of the ascending soul to its new home. First farewell in silence, alone with her. The second takes place a week later at a Christian-Hindu service for her.

The end of a family story. Nobody there any more. Now it has happened.

As if the loss of the mother wasn't enough of an intense, painful experience of life, his life partner moves out the day after the service for the mother. While this was no surprise, was in fact expected, the coincidence of events stretches the pain potential for our affected brother by several orders of magnitude.

To lose a loved one through natural death is painful because it is irretrievable, that person is permanently lost to this world. As a natural process mourning is the appropriate emotional reaction to it. To give up a living person without wanting it, one you love with all your heart, is painful in a different way and stabs deep into the heart. What emotions has nature provided for such cases? Grief is not it. "Melancholy" is too weakly formulated. Rather, it is depression, anxiety and panic. A pain cocktail without equal. It can break a man who has no psychological resistance or spiritual practice. Many a suicide has had just such a cause. There's not a powerful Job[14] in everyone.

So much regarding these events. The person concerned is, thank God, a Vedantin.

---

14 In the Book of Job in the Old Testament of the Bible, Job had all family members taken through death as a test of loyalty to God. Contrary to the prediction and the expectations of Satan, Job remains faithful to his Lord God despite an infinity of painful inner struggles. C. G. Jung has worked through this story using depth psychology in " Antwort auf Hiob", "Answer to Job", published among others, by Walter Publishing House. In German the expression 'Job's tidings' means tidings about a very terrible event.

Spiritual processing of pain:

"An Indian knows no pain" – we used to shout as children, after minor injuries and quarrels. However, it's not quite as simple as this for the Indians. They certainly know pain, but handle it differently to a non-Indian. The latter is a synonym for a psychologically and spiritually inexperienced person. The 'Indian' stands for the more advanced person.

The easiest trick to take power away from pain is to withdraw the attention from the pain sensation. This works perfectly, even with violent toothaches. However, it takes some practice in concentration, discipline and mindfulness. With emotional pain this trick doesn't work so well. Emotions sit deeper in a person than muscles, organs, or the nervous system. Emotions are subtle in nature and accordingly can only be reached on a subtle mental level. Our consciousness does have such possibilities by being able to change the thinking patterns, or by modification of the communication within the mind (Manas). To this end, there is again need for training or even psychotherapy with the help of professionals. The well-intentioned friendly advice "All is well" or "It'll be all right", although communicating a sense of belonging and participation, is usually not sufficient for effective pain processing or resolution.

What possibilities are available to the spiritually advanced student for dealing with stress and pain processing?

An experienced Yogi[15] has, first of all, a rich repertoire of exercises addressing physiological-energetic aspects, known as Asanas, Pranayama, and relaxation. Or he may practice rituals that delve into prayer, or he may sink his mind into contemplation and the silence of meditation.

---

15 Somebody who practices some form of traditional yoga, such as Ashtanga, Hatha or other forms of practical energy yoga.

A Bhakta[16] converses with Vishnu or the Divine Mother Shakti as did Ramakrishna with the utmost fervor. He undertakes, so to speak, a two-way interaction with the higher powers. When an advanced and humble Bhakta enters this interaction it is not a fiction, a simple cinema of the imagination, but an authentic, transcendental encounter. What is commonly and rather casually referred to as 'inner guidance' occurs as a reality in the sphere of consciousness of those seeking advice and solace in such a spiritualized situation.

The inexpressible anchors itself in the consciousness and helps the being to reach a grounded stabilization of emotions. Such an invocation must be considered a much more subtle process than can be provided by the psychological and subtle nature of the emotional world. The cosmic law is that an influence always proceeds effectively from the subtle to the gross.

A Jnani[17] has a number of integral possibilities. He can engage the mind, influence the emotions, contact the gods[18] or enter the silence of the Heart. In all of this, he knows that he is not the one who feels the pain, it is the mind-body system. Admittedly this sounds somewhat mechanical, but basically the Jnani sees it that way. He values the body and all the energetic possibilities of earthly existence as instruments of action and also uses them just like any other human being. However, he does not identify with this instrument physically, mentally, or emotionally, but remains as a witness, the observer of all processes.

But here again we should remain realistic regarding the actual ability to reach such an elevated level of consciousness. Many con-

---

16 See glossary!

17 See glossary!

18 In Advaita Vedanta as a Nondual Teaching, the gods exist as real beings in the cosmic level of Brahmaloka. Despite the two-way communication with them, the Jnani is always aware that ultimately all advice comes from the Self, the Atman.

temporary Neo-Advaita teachers simplify human life and all its processes, including the coping strategies. Even enlightenment is not an issue, it is very easy. "You're already there, it's never been otherwise" – one hears this in some seminars going around in echoing and suggestively repetitive tones. From the absolute point of view this is so, however, 99 percent of the billions of fallen angels do not actually have access to this highest recognition[19]. If the enlightenment process were as simple as pronounced by some of the protagonists of these new doctrines of salvation in the guise of classical teachings, our Mother Earth would be teeming with enlightened ones. But is that so? Just look around more closely. The answer is obvious. Such frivolous promises must always be viewed critically.

Whether beginner or advanced, we have the possibility of creating an inner distance from states of mind. However, it requires a clear inner alignment. We must be deeply convinced that we are not the body, not the feelings and not the thinker. These are the indispensible qualifications of a Vedantic aspirant. Without having internalized these Vedantic principles, the student will not progress. Let us emphasize again that these are not just mental assumptions, but are aspects of the multi-millennial Tradition and of unchanged great mysteries, as delineated in the non-dual metaphysics of Advaita Vedanta.

Practically seen, the realm of experience of an (advanced) Jnani – taking the case of intense pain described in the beginning of this chapter – would look something like this:

The Jnani (as a woman or man) is permanently situated in a dichotomous consciousness, present on two levels. (Please do not confuse this with schizoid states!) One level is the normal sphere

---

19 Recognition in Advaita is synonymous with realization, the vision of God, liberation. It is a non-mental event – supernatural, as measured by worldly standards.

of the physical-mental-emotional experience. Here the pain is felt intensely, depending on the available degree of coping, as already described. At level two, on the other hand, there is no pain and no emotion, not even a thought. This level is beyond the mundane, and is not part of the normal world, but the cause of it. It is of Universal nature and it manifests as Buddhi-Principle[20] for the being existing in this manifest world.

Ultimately, it is Atman that observes. As the direct reflection of the absolute Brahman, he remains as unaffected by all the events of the relative worlds as the cinema screen is unaffected by the play of lights on its surface.

Depending on where the advanced Jnani puts his momentary focus of attention, he experiences the pain, or he can watch it untouched by it. Ramana Maharshi had always recommended the question: "Who is it who is experiencing the pain, to whose awareness does it come?" as Vichara exercise. This can be asked by anyone regardless of their basic spiritual orientation, and the practitioner will experience the miracle of inner distance. A new freedom, serenity and detachment will gradually set in. The pain will not continue to dominate him, but rather, the practitioner will now be master in his own house of inner spirituality.

This method can be applied not only to pain, but is recommended as a general spiritual principle of how to look at oneself, life and the world. In this way a permanent process of approaching the Self begins. It ends in meditation in Savikalpa or Nirvikalpa Samadhi[21]. A sudden, unmediated and unexpected higher influence can likewise take place in the serious and humble seeker of truth. With a mighty bolt of lightning and thunder, the ego and the lower self dissolves in the ocean of eternity.

---

20 see Buddhi in glossary!
21 state of Samadhi see glossary!

Unfortunately, this event cannot be demanded, nor planned, nor forced, nor solicited. The mind finds it downright fantastic and exciting that there is something higher than itself. It wants to get to know it. Let's have it now! And fast! So thinks the erring Western (small) mind. The Yogi knows that enlightenment can neither be an object of thought or anticipation. It cannot even be desperately wished for. All of this doesn't help. The unthinkable cannot be put into words, phrases, or images. And beyond the unthinkable we cannot think. So how can this mystical approach to the Divine take place at all?

Martin Luther, that very courageous reformer of the early 16th Century, expressed it with the previously mentioned principle of "sola fide". That is, "by faith alone" - or "sola gratia", "by grace alone" – does man attain heaven and thus cleansed, appear before the Lord. But even in Luther's sense grace may be granted only to the cleansed, which means the qualified.

We therefore have no choice but to work on ourselves thoroughly, no matter what great doctrine we subscribe to. Student qualifications don't happen with just knowledge from books or attending seminars, but only through hard, continuous practice and in a constant struggle for apperception through Vichara (self-inquiry), Viveka (higher intuitively intelligent discrimination) and Vairagya (mental renunciation of the cosmos of the relative, permanent internal detachment).

These qualities cannot be stressed often enough, and the reader may forgive us if we repeat them often in this book. Shankara argues very insistently for student qualifications in works such as Drigdrisyaviveka, Atmabodha or Vivekacudamani. For Ramakrishna it was dedication and devotion, worship and ritual as Bhakti qualifications. As a classical Advaitin Raphael teaches the unity of consciousness and awareness of the importance of the great

Mahavakya[22] Tat Tvam Asi (you [Self] are That [Supreme]) as well as the unity of Eastern and Western initiation teachings. He also thus emphasizes the need to qualify on each path.

Naturally one can also hold to the emphatic recommendation of Ramesh Balsekar and other Neo-Advaita teachers, and postulate: you cannot do anything. You have no will of your own, you are not the one who steers your destiny. This means: you are powerless in the play of God. "Where there is nothing, nothing can be missing," says the title of one of his last books. Following Balsekar's absolutist view, there is no ego that acts, and therefore you have to leave everything to the higher cosmic law, which created the world and life far from our influence. It should be strongly emphasized that with the greatest respect for Ramesh this is not the classical Advaita Vedanta of a Gaudapada, Govindapada and Shankara, but a form of selective truth from the Shruti[23]23. He is thus increasingly removed from our point of view and also from that of his master Nisargadatta, who was much closer to the classical-original Advaita.

Conclusion for the processing of spiritual pain:

There is no spiritual pain. With increasing qualifications the spiritual human being is increasingly unassailable, and less subject to worldly processes, whether in the personal-psychological field or from events in the outside world. The loss of a person, whether through death or separation, is dealt with differently from people in normal society. However, pain is felt when consciousness is present in the lower state, ie; in the ego - Manas system. If there is a possibility of transcending the lower self for the person involved, then the person finds himself in the witness consciousness, which is without distress and anguish. This latter is usually the high state of a Teacher-Master, but advanced students may also partially and

22 Mahavakya: see Glosssary!

23 Shruti, the Revealed Divine, not conceived by human knowledge-recognition.

temporarily evoke this state. In this way a certain distance takes place, which allows for greater serenity and detachment from conflicts and problems. These are rare and unusual possibilities within the spectrum of human experience, because only in this state does it first become possible to escape the world and its events through distance and renunciation. The Karma not only changes towards the positive, but towards dissolution.

For the classical Advaitin precisely this is "The Path of Fire" as Raphael calls it, the Holy Fire of Shivaic dissolution and renewal.

May all beings find this cosmic pearl of God.

OM TAT SAT – Shanti

5. Everyday Life Claims Me Repeatedly

Conversion out of nowhere

After an apprenticeship as a technical electrician filled with stress and characterized by a devastated self-esteem, a distinct reversal, as it were all by itself, appeared in my inner being while I was still a very young teen-ager. It was true that I had been confirmed a Protestant and on that path had virtuously attended all the church services as was ordered. Nonetheless, the sermons almost always bounced completely off me. Nothing of them reached me. In any case, without any exterior motivation I started an intensive Bible study. Only now, years after the influence of the church, was it possible for me to become a Christian in the true sense of the Gospel. But certainly not in the way it is presented by or pretended to by the church organization. Because I was working during the day the Bible became my nightly bedtime reading. A must before going to sleep. I read completely through the Old and New Testament. And not just once. I was most fascinated by the first book of Moses (Genesis) with the creation and origins stories, and in particular Abraham, who out of love and devotion to God (Vedanta: Bhakti) had almost killed his own son, and the Sermon on the Mount (Matthew 5-7 or Luke 6, 20-49), the content of which includes everything needed to guide and direct a sincere Christian, one who is interested solely in the pure message of Christ.

I began to "preach" in private circles with fervor and conviction. Even work colleagues were not safe from my well-meaning spiritual waves of enthusiasm. After a while some began to make fun of me, calling out "Ah, here comes our Jesus again" as soon as I entered the workshop. Still, it was amazing to me that many listened, even the scoffers and in particular older colleagues of about forty. I myself was not yet twenty.

At that time, and as an act of pure grace, those spiritual roots manifested in my heart that still today provide me with a source of strength and of spiritual nourishment for the understanding. At an event by the American evangelist Billy Graham, my almost missionary ambitions received their strongest confirmation to date, which I was able to experience, completely fascinated, in the sold-out Dortmund Westfalen hall. Despite the necessary translations into German, this extraordinary man lost nothing of his charisma and persuasiveness. At the end of the event, people flooded in their thousands to the lower part of the hall, and were converted anew by Billy. At that time seeing baptized Christians converted by one who does not belong to their church, was for me incredibly poignant, thrilling, and enthralling. Now fully convinced of the high, vibrant radiance of religion in the midst of a materialistic age, I later studied theology, among other things, with a focus on comparative religion.

Since then I have learned a very important lesson: it's true that the world does get to you with its claims and oftentimes drastic distractions, caused by problems and pleasures, but once a spiritual seed has begun to sprout, then the being always has recourse to the strengths that develop with it.

During the work on this book very dramatic and cataclysmic events were happening in the world. The people of the North African states of Egypt, Yemen, Libya and others stood up and revolted against their oppressive regimes, fighting and risking their lives for Western-style democracies. Primarily it is the youth who have developed this new and incredibly powerful force. The old admire this and are ashamed, as it were, that they have not achieved this in their time. But now the "Arab Spring" has arrived.

The people of these mainly Islamic countries live their religion in everyday life more intensely than the average Christian of the West. For them, it is unthinkable to separate their God Allah from everyday events. They draw their strength from a quasi-double source: from the political force released against an enduring oppression and from their own living religion. A Vedantin finds such a consistent and sincerely integrated attitude to spirituality wonderful, as long as it remains peaceful. Here you see an integrated and holistic life shining through. The "Arab Spring" holds a tremendous transformative power in its collective heart. These courageous people should have every possible support from the European countries.

How do we in the West link spirituality with everyday life? This simple question has a very serious background, far more serious than it may appear at first glance. Why serious? Because the spiritual orientation of a person determines the entire modality of their life-course and their life after physical death. Can there be anything more important in life? Of course, readers of a book on Advaita have already more or less extensively dealt with this issue. But how do they manage to translate any knowledge gained into the practice of life? Now, I do not mean how often someone drags himself to meditation, prayer or contemplation, but rather, I ask about the mindfulness and awareness of what we ARE.

We can learn, one might even say "practice", to be aware of our true nature every second of the day until sleep occurs. If the awareness just once rises in us, powerfully and clearly, that we are not actually the body, not the mind-intellect, not the emotions - but soul, Jivatman-Atman, then it is possible to gradually dispose of the daily events of life with little or few identifications, even though one is in the midst of them. This applies equally to what is thought, what is felt, the behavior, outer events and internal scenarios.

Sometimes, however, external events are extremely violent, as can be seen in the example of the recent Arab liberation efforts and in another event that took place at the same time, in those days of March, 2011: the unimaginably dramatic natural disaster in Japan. Earthquakes up to magnitude 9.0, giant tsunamis over 15 meters high, huge fires, and to make matters still worse, as a result of these natural forces, reactor accidents in nuclear power plants with unpredictable effects on people living far away. Helpless thousands lost their lives. Radioactivity contaminated the sea and the air.

In view of such extreme degrees of suffering and harm the mind quite rightly wonders how could it succeed in not identifying. If non-identification is used synonymously with coolness, indifference, unconcern or impassivity, then naturally a compassionately oriented consciousness cannot agree to it. Any genuine spiritual seeker-aspirant feels compassion for other sentient beings, and as well, constantly and independently of pleasure or pain. And, of course, one should help wherever one can within ones limitations. The Vedanta Teacher has, however, always forcefully pointed out that in terms of Karma Yoga man should not understand himself to be the doer, but that everything be left to God. The understandable and natural human question regarding disasters, why a compassionate God can allow such proportions of destruction, arises from our instilled concepts of morality and ethics and cannot be answered satisfactorily from this point of view. During those dramatic days of the natural disaster in Japan a German Catholic monsignor who works in a Christian mission in Egypt said something very interesting in a radio interview (paraphrased):

> *We can perhaps begin to see that we do not belong to this earth, at best we are guests. But this world is not paradise. We exploit nature and do not understand what we are causing here. We must bow to the forces of nature and find our own spiritual alignment. The question of the role of God in such events is of secondary importance. We must learn to come to terms with the power of His creative force.*

From the standpoint of Advaita we can add that both the creative (Brahma) and sustaining (Vishnu) as well as the destructive (Shiva) forces influence the Universe. However, we must address a common misconception about the function of Shiva. In the Hindu Trimurti doctrine (similar to the Christian Trinity) Shiva does not have the role of a destroyer in the sense of disdainful destruction but as a Destroyer-Renewer. From the naive Christian perspective Shiva would compare with the devil, the originator and highest representative of evil. But it is just the opposite of this. He is the supreme Guru, the Guru of all Gurus, the manifestation of love and compassion, and in Shankara's Advaita as renewer. He has extraordinary importance for the liberation of the being from the yoke of the egoic individuality.

Without the Shivaic force of destruction-renewal human beings have no chance of liberation, salvation and enlightenment. They would endlessly slip from existence to existence without a glimmer of hope. This Shivaic power lies dormant in every human being. Should it mature to full awakening, man then gives up his old, small, ego-driven personality and awakens to a new life, which proceeds according to completely different principles. As Jesus aptly said: whosoever wants to reach the kingdom of heaven must first be born again.

It may happen that within a master-disciple relationship of the Vedantic lineage a disciple gets a new name from the master. A name that corresponds to his newly achieved level of consciousness after having received many initiations and Darshanas and having reached a certain level of maturity on the spiritual ladder. This new human being is only fragmentarily related to the old, familiar personality. Only the physical sheath is still similar (but not the same, because it is constantly changing). Even this is deceptive, because essential changes have taken place in the subtle sheaths as a result of the transcendental unfolding that gradually acts from inside to outside. Thanks to the power of Shiva and the guru's love and grace a very subtle but comprehensive and revolutionary renewal process has taken place, one which has little in common with all the previously lived lives of former existences, although all were in fact preparing for the moment of clear insight.

From these contexts Shankara's Vedantic guideline can be clearly seen: that one should not judge a teacher-master by his visible actions. Because, unlike with less developed people, under and behind these events pure Karma Yoga takes place - the attitudes of love-devotion of Bhakti and clear recognition–discrimination of Jnana. This is not easy to understand and more particularly to accept, because all too often we hear of pseudo-gurus attempting to gain a carte blanche for their misconduct by citing their guru status, or radical cult leaders who torment their devotees, have sex with them and by using blackmail force them into total dependence.

All of this has absolutely nothing in common with the holy One Tradition. However, abuse will always exist, especially in the Kali Yuga. The sincere student must be all the more vigilant not to be sucked into a merciless trap by a charismatic teacher with velvety voice.

A genuine teacher and master true to the line of the Advaita Vedanta tradition will never force his followers to do anything, manipulate or seduce them, bind them emotionally, influence them subconsciously-suggestively, impress them with Siddhi powers, threaten them, and the like. He removes the person from the foreground and represents the teaching exclusively. What person should he place in the foreground? The normal human version actually no longer exists. In modern computer parlance the transcended person is an upgrade of the old person. The old person exists only in fragments within the renewed being.

Karl Pribram, John C. Eccles, the great philosopher and theoretician of science Karl Raimund Popper and some other researchers of consciousness have created their own term for this. When there is an unforeseen leap of an evolutionary nature in spirit-endowed beings, we speak of "emergence". This is not directly comparable with other phenomena, such as mutation in biology, but is a purely spiritual event that brings forth totally new and great extensions of intelligence and knowledge.

Seen from this standpoint the state of enlightenment in Samadhi is an emergent phenomenon that cannot - solely - be explained as the sum of the many practical and theoretical preparations, but is a leap into a world of different dimensions, a plane of existence far beyond the physical universe. More scientifically formulated: it is a plane that is causal to the physical. In yet other words, it is the world of pure being, from which the gross-material world appears. It is the causal realm for the levels of becoming (Samsara).

Perhaps it is now a little more clear to the reader how closely and finely woven the subtle and gross material worlds are intertwined. Therefore, for the Advaitin there is no real separation between everyday life and Sadhana, between the daily experiences in and with society and those in the meditation. The fundamental law of the

One Tradition "All is One!" only achieves its irrevocable meaning if this One is almost completely - or even very briefly - experienced. And if this is the case, then this being stands on the threshold to the Universal. Everything is then seen only from this perspective of Oneness. The multiplicity loses more and more and is being replaced by an all-encompassing world-view. The dual vanishes, mine and thine dissolve, the 'I' and 'you' merge to I or I Am. Such an emergence experience anchors the essence deep in being and causes all doubts about God, eternity and bliss (Satchidananda in Advaita) to blow away like dandelion seeds in a strong wind. Certainty rather timid faith sets in, as well as peace, tranquility and equanimity.

From my diverse experience as a human resources manager of a company and as an executive coach, I know how things are internally structured for the majority of people in working life. The vast majority is not interested in spiritual topics. They not only defend themselves from such, but judge and condemn spiritual people as cranks and irrational, morbid neurotics and esoteric dreamers. The seeker they regard simply as someone who wants to escape their so-called reality, and can't make it because they are too weak. "loser", "weakling", "coward", "sectarian" are common labels. The materialist world-view of the twenty-first century is still very much in the minds of the masses. The real is supposedly the visible and tangible, as that with which the relevant experience can be made, something concrete, logical and rational or physically comprehensible.

Such emphasis on the superficial-empirical is understandable if we look at the conditioning apparatus of man, the subconscious. It has been shaped through world spans and over eons. These seemingly real experiences have left impressions upon the soft, wax-like sediment of the subconscious mind; in psychic natural law they have the function of anchoring experiences in the reservoir of consciousness of the being and to make them retrievable at any time.

Whoever hasn't yet understood exactly what we are talking about here, and who would like to imagine how it is, or even better to try it out, switch right now from your main hand to the other, your secondary hand, and now try to do everything that was done with the main hand with the other. A right-hander now writes with the left, or even with his feet or with his mouth. Place the pen between your toes or clamp it in your mouth, and have a go! The example of severely disabled people who need to use other body parts shows the fact that wonderful results can indeed be achieved in this way. With the very first try you'll see just how difficult such a switch is to someone who has been conditioned otherwise.

The great spiritual Masters point out that it is impossible to empty this powerful reservoir of conditioning with normal, empirical means of effort. It would amount to the same absurd attempt as sitting on a beach with a teaspoon to empty the ocean. The content of the stored experiences of the subconscious and the two other types of consciousness, the individual and collective unconscious[24], is so vast and inconceivable in the multi-faceted dimensions of the impressions that any ever-so-diligent effort at illumination is doomed from the beginning to fail. Even, and especially, psycho-analytic methods don't even come close. No one could possibly lie on the famous couch for so long. Only a serious spirituality, well-founded in an initiatiory tradition can make the seemingly impossible possible: liberation from the despotic straitjacket of the sub- and unconscious layers. This is tantamount to saying goodbye to the world of becoming (Samsara), and is only possible within a

---

24 In scientific psychology, there is the division into conscious, sub-and unconscious. The great student of Freud, C. G. Jung, created the concept of the collective unconscious based on his own research. These are the experiences of all humanity, which can be expressed as the archetypes, energetic symbol contents in dreams. In Vedanta we recognize in addition the individual unconscious, which is the reservoir of all previous lives of Jivatma, the individualized soul.

spirituality that is systematically and continuously practiced under the guidance of a qualified teacher / guru.

Once the spark of truth has leapt to the aspirant and his consciousness has taken it in, then there is neither an excuse for skipping spiritual exercises based on the pressures of everyday life, nor a way back on this road of no return. This being is now well and truly on the way and is a blessing to all who come in contact with him.

The fire of The Path of Fire
cannot be extinguished!

6. Modern Life Phases and Spirituality

As laid out in the Vedas, in Hinduism there are four stages in life (Ashramas), which the seeker of Truth goes through:

1. The student of Brahma (Brahmacharya)
2. The householder (Grihastha)
3. The forest hermit (Vanaprastha)
4. The wandering ascetic (Samnyasa or Sannyasa)

The life of a spiritual man is divided in these four stages. They give him clear guidelines with the ultimate goal of Realization – which may not necessarily be reached in this present lifetime. These are not political or socially oriented directives that somebody has made up, but come from the Vedas themselves and from the Upanishads. Thus they belong to Shruti, the sacred revelations, and as such may also be examined for their suitability for Western man. For the truth is not a privilege of the East. Let us simply examine each stage individually. On the basis of the descriptions in the Tradition we can then examine our life situations in the West and see, looked at from the perspective of the old directives, if they are still suitable.

The central theme of each life stage is spiritual self-realization. The stages in life are intended to help prepare for it effectively. In the West there are at least three different perspectives for viewing self-realization. We shall review each one of them before we examine the four life stages so we avoid any misunderstanding.

- **Self-realization in the private sphere and work environment**

  Here we mean personal freedom, which is possible for a human being within a society. This addresses creative processes in the work environment as well as in the domestic-private area. If in a person's life there are sufficient possibilities in both areas to fully live out his abilities, desires, goals, hobbies and passions, this is then understood as self-realization. The basic criterion here is the presence of feelings with a tendency towards contentment. If this sense of well-being is reached the person tends to leave everything as it is. Because of the appearance of well-being one does not investigate any further growth in psychological and spiritual directions. There is very little to object to with such a positive experience, except that it is by nature totally transient, without substance, subject to constant change, and always overshadowed by the anxiety of losing it. People who are immersed in a collective trend of a society or who just drift along practice this kind of self-realization without getting to question life itself. Only through shock, illness and encounters with death do they get shaken up enough to begin to contemplate the fundamental questions of life and its impermanence, but in most cases usually only for a short while.

- **Psychological Self-Realization**

  Many decades ago the great humanistic psychologist Abraham Maslow developed the concept of a hierarchy of needs pyramid. It starts with basic needs (physiological), then above that are social needs and the top represents self-actualization. Here the focus is on the mind-ego-emotions-system (in Advaita: Ahamkara-Manas) where the basic needs are met, the social and cultural-artistic needs are satisfied and through repeated critical self-analysis a state of peaceful and amicable serenity is reached. This state in turn can better deal with stress and conflicts and can take responsibility on the social and personal level by incorporating higher values including the element of soul.

Far fewer people reach this form of self-realization than in the first case. One of the reasons for this is the significant lack of willingness to undergo self-critique as well as a lack of the capacity for critical reflection. The ego downright forbids such a self-analysis, because it would run the risk of losing its absolute sense of grandeur, which maintains its distinct and clear separation from others. Its perceived sense of uniqueness and the constructed personality, which has been dynamically created from birth onwards, would have to suffer losses that could not be tolerated. At least not without a crisis. And who wants to enter an identity crisis voluntarily? So, no self-examinations! Feedback from outside is equally vehemently avoided or rejected aggressively on the verbal level. Depending on the temperament 'hiding maneuvers' are also possible, with the word 'escape' inscribed on the banner, thus avoiding all that is uncomfortable.

People who engage seriously in psychological self-realization are already on a much higher level of existence than those within the mass consciousness with its material-social priorities. Surprisingly, there are business enterprises and public authorities that embrace this theme within their company philosophies and recommend related seminars to their upper management. However, what is actually put into practice from what is heard and learned is another question, which can be best discovered in the literature from the relevant department in the companies.

- **Spiritual Self-Realization**

  On closer inspection it becomes clear that the renaissance of the integration of the soul into the life of Western man has been happening only for the last 30 – 40 years. Aside from the Christian churches, the Beatles' guru Maharishi Mahesh Yogi, Bhagawan, later also known as Osho, Krishnamurti, Ramana Maharshi and other great souls such as Vivekananda and Paramahansa Yogananda, to mention just a few, acted as motors and catalysts to inspire an interest for spiritual themes amongst the wider population.

  In this kind of self-realization the being longs for complete dissolution of the ego-Manas complex in order to transform itself from the individual into the Universal. In the psychological sub-category we have already mentioned the fear of self-criticism. Here it is not just about criticism, but about the death of the ego, its total dissolution. It is quite obvious that only a few human beings are ready for this. Shankara emphasizes in his Sutras that amongst 1,000 people only a very few strive to reach perfection, and amongst these few only one is capable of knowing God (realizing God).

  In that regard nothing has changed since the times of Shankaracharya. On the contrary, the situation has rather changed for the worse in the centuries since his teaching. On one hand it has worsened through poverty, wars, and epidemics and on the other hand through the increasing affluence of the last 150 years, which has led people into ever-greater delusions through its multiplicity of comforts.

  A spiritual teacher within an authentic initiatory tradition is aware of the current situation. Because of that he is not concerned with having a large number of students, but devotedly

> looks after a few with the necessary qualifications, who are willing to dedicate as much sincerity, patience and perseverance as is necessary. When the Karma is ripe the disciple and the teacher find each other miraculously, without any effort.

Now let us return to the classic life stages of Hinduism.

The first stage: Brahmacharya

According to the classical view in Hinduism, in the first stage the young person acquires knowledge in worldly and religious affairs through instruction by his parents and teachers. The emphasis is on the development of his thinking, feeling and actions as virtues for a spiritual life. Ideally, he would already now have contact with a spiritual teacher-master (guru) who guides him on the path of knowledge of Brahma (Brahmajnana). The teacher can help him to re-awaken the hidden realization within him or at least make all the essential preparations for it.

This includes attitudes, behavior and values such as celibacy, abstinence (Vairagya) and chastity. All the five senses are to be focused on these virtues and even the sixth sense, the thinking. This indicates that this education is primarily concerned with a future monastic life. But it is certainly also useful for a spiritual life practice and its further transmission to his descendants, if there is marriage in the next stage.

Already at this first stage the focus is to develop higher discernment (Viveka), which will help avoid shallow entertainment and not let oneself be influenced too strongly by either joy or grief. Regular spiritual practice develops the potential of higher intelligence (Buddhi) as the beginning of the 'manasic' disintegration process (elimination of the lower intellect). This means that the lower intelligence of the Manas will gradually become re-absorbed into the higher Buddhi.

How does this life stage present itself to the modern Western man?

Parents, kindergarten, school, training and adult education devote an enormous effort towards the preparation and criteria for an appropriate social survival in the Western Hemisphere. Religious education is also in the curriculum, however it is dealt with like a fifth wheel. If somebody excels in sport and religion but otherwise has average grades he does not qualify as an achiever or a person on whom the society pins its hopes. In addition to that there is the hesitant or negative attitude towards religion within the practice of everyday life. Prayers at the table or before going to bed have become rare these days. Only in times of despair and distress, due to illness, death or accident does one turn again towards God, who then should, please, come and help. But otherwise only 'the psychological comfort', as my Master calls it, through prosperity and consumerism, counts as relevant and makes life worth living.

Granted, this picture might be a little pessimistic. Certainly, even in our society there are other viewpoints. However, upon closer inspection one discovers even far more drastic materialistic and atheistic attitudes. The affluent man of our times has dedicated himself to illusion (Maya). He identifies with his body and with his possessions. He has been brain-washed that to accumulate and to possess a lot will make him satisfied – and he believes it. But since everything is constantly changing, the desires endless and nothing permanent, he chases after happiness all his life. If he is poor he chases primarily after imaginary dream goals, if he is rich he is terrified of losing his possessions.

Deep-rooted equanimity towards possessions, adversity, pleasure and pain as well as health comes about only if the person has ignited and is feeling the fire of transcendental life within. Autogenic training and other psycho-physiological relaxation techniques can help as an introduction to bring the body-feeling-mind system into balance. But we must not stop there. As in the case of the Brahmacharin one should take up the intensive study of the sacred texts and find a group of people (Satsangha) with which to initiate the steps of spiritual survival and orientate towards God and the transformation of the lower self.

The life stage of a Brahmacharya can be adopted at any time and at any age during a lifetime. It may safely be regarded as one of the most essential decisions or steps in a person's life. A step in the direction of the actual purpose of human beings: to come back to the source of our origin. Precisely this is the meaning of religion. This source is on one hand far beyond any thought and all ideas. On the other hand it is closer than the breath. It is guarded as a hidden treasure in a tiny chamber in our hearts.

The second stage (Grihastha)

In Hinduism this is the stage of a householder and a family father. Here the person fulfills his social duties by marriage and the rearing of children. Marriage is not considered a union for convenience, but a spiritual exercise, and it has a profound spiritual dimension in the shaping of consciousness through the union of Yin and Yang elements of man and woman.

The significant lessons are: self-control, compassion, deferment of ones own desires, observance of social sensitivities, all the way to altruism (giving without expecting to receive back or be appreciated). Of course, all of this is based on all the values of a Brahmacharya. Children are seen as blessings, because they represent the link between life and death and ensure the survival of the culture. When a boy has reached the age of 12 he can act in his father's place as head of the family.

The word 'Ashram' has evolved from the fact that the family father retreats to the solitude of the forest together with his wife, so he can devote himself to the study of the Holy Scriptures and the meditation in order to achieve liberation (Moksha) from the world of becoming (Samsara). Even to this day an ashram is a place where one dedicates oneself to religious studies and to meditation and contemplation. In addition to the proverbial cave in the Himalayas, this can be a house in the country, a communal retreat facility, a hermitage or a monastery.

Because the Vedic elements of the life stages build upon each other it is clear that the father and his wife behave as Brahmacharyas and so integrate the values of the first stage completely into their lives as a couple and as parents.

How can one transfer these humanistic-transpersonal ways of life into the Western world?

'Alienation' is a word coined by Karl Marx to describe the loss of the self-initiated, satisfying work and life style by industrialized, monotonous life processes, which increasingly distance man from his natural being as a self-determining human being. How right he was. Today both work and consumerism keep us from our true purpose.

These days who wants to hear anything about renunciation and detachment? That would mean abstaining from a very pleasant lifestyle. Perhaps even abstaining from prosperity? No, the normal person is not willing to do that. And why should he, if life can be more comfortable? This common opinion contains a series of errors and misunderstandings. Raphael explains this in his commentary on Vivekacudamani[25]:

---

25 (see Raphael, Vivekacudamini, Bielefeld 2004, p. 56 f.)

There are no limits on the level of detachment; ranging from the insignificant object to the detachment from the dearest friend, from a family member to Brahma[26]*. All the great sages have said: If you want to follow the path of the spirit you have to 'leave everything behind', even your children, parents and personal ideals... Of course, the detachment should not happen as a reaction to something, nor as a repression or an irrational imposing of something upon oneself, but has to happen as a consequence of a profound, logical and intuitive insight... Any detachment, which has not matured out of a deep inner understanding, is not a true insight.*

For a Western mind this is rather strong stuff, almost unattainable, it seems even contemptuous of human beings, dismissive, unfriendly, anti-social, comparable to an extremely radical outsider. And that is supposed to be a recommendation of a holy teaching? Who, for heaven's sake, can identify with something like that? That would be equivalent to isolating oneself, becoming lonely and excluded from society. Can this be taken seriously or is there something hiding behind it unrecognized?

Indeed, something is hiding behind this detachment (Vairagya). It's about detachment, which does not mean unconditional giving up of everything. In principle and greatly abridged it means: you can use all the amenities of modern affluent life, however you may on no account get attached to anything in such a way that you might think you would not be able to live without it. You have to be free from bonds, free from any attachment. This applies to all areas of life, the material, social, psychological, imaginary, cultural, family, yes, even the spiritual.

---

26 first Godhead of Trimurti, Brahma, Vishnu, Shiva (note of the author)

The second stage in life is a training ground for learning to not even cling to the spiritual. The attachment to the goal of 'liberation' is intrinsically wrong. One can't strive for liberation, we have mentioned this repeatedly before. However, the thought of this goal should permeate our entire being and resound in the subconscious like a permanent echo, allowing an inner transformation to happen, while the spiritual practice strengthens it energetically.

Contemporary Advaita teachers who do not follow the classical Tradition exhibit to their followers a life that is quite indulgent and sexually active, exactly demonstrating this notion that one can enjoy everything if one is not attached. It raises a serious doubt, however, of whether this is didactically appropriate and an effective model for a path of liberation. A Grihastha may live with all the possibilities that he may have available, but he lives a greatly simplified life, always preferring the simple to the luxurious. That is not difficult for him, because he does not lack anything. He has all that he needs to survive, more is not necessary.

Shankara reminds us actually that the spiritual seeker needs two very important circumstances for spiritual progress: prosperity and health. If he is not sufficiently provided for and lives in abject poverty his entire consciousness will be filled with thoughts of food and shelter. If the person has not been sufficiently prepared spirituality moves completely into the background. If one is not healthy, feels miserable, sick and weak, spiritual practice is not possible because the thoughts will be automatically focused on physical survival. A balance is necessary between prosperity and health. In Shankara's terminology prosperity means to have available everything necessary for life, but in simplicity. And health is a state of homeostasis, the dynamic equilibrium of all biological and psychological forces.

The reader of these lines may now ask himself to what extent and in what areas of his own life may change be possible and should make every effort to reach a clearer focus for an existence in spiritual freedom. He ultimately attains freedom from all constrains, concerns and fears.

Once you have tasted the liberating nectar of the Universal Gods (Brahmaloka), what is there to be afraid of?

The third stage (Vanaprastha)

The Vanaprastha, it is true, has left behind the first two life stages, but still continues to live and shape the values of the first stages by completely withdrawing from social life and dedicating himself entirely to liberation from his karmic bonds. As already mentioned, this can be done together with his wife or life partner. Today there are many alternatives to the cave in the Himalayas. The reclusiveness serves to fundamentally cultivate solitude through an in-depth spiritual practice (Sadhana).

In his heart the Vanaprastha increasingly feels the non-reality of all dualistic opposites. He deliberately practices Vairagya, he detaches himself from all desires of the relative world and from all its associated attachments. He strictly avoids turbulent and heavily populated places. Due to his natural and benign detachment from all the hustle and bustle he can be a helpful coach and advisor, who, should he be asked for help, can administer to the problems of others objectively. His simple, innocent, liberated and spiritually practical way of life (doing Japa and Dhyana, recitation of Mantras and meditation) provides those seeking advice with a meaningful role model for a life of inner freedom.

Part of it is also observing proper dietary guidelines. First and foremost it is crucial to have a balanced, mainly vegetarian, Sattvic diet[27], which is more energizing and more pure than the nor-

---

27 Sattva is the highest of the three Gunas (fundamental principles of nature) Tamas as lethargic, Rajas as (hyper) active and Sattva as rarefied balance of the other two Gunas. Sattva belongs to the Universal or it is the gateway to it. In Vedic Hinduism food is classified and described according to the Gunas.

mal diet consisting of heavily cooked food and meat and fish. In his scriptures Swami Sivananda recommends such Sattvic food as: milk, cereals, butter, cheese, tomatoes, honey, fruit, sweets, barley, wheat, dates and almonds.

As Avatar Lord Krishna recommends, spicy, too hot, bitter, sour, and salty food should be avoided. This is Rajasic food for those who are attached to passions. Everything that is stale, tasteless, spoiled, rotten and impure is considered Tamasic food.

People who are on the spiritual path should primarily consume the Sattvic diet. Food is matter and it vibrates. This vibration connects with the vibration within the body and can be beneficial, or it can interfere and even harm. This is why it is recommended to observe the appropriate vibrational spectrum in regard to our food. That way spiritual evolution can happen more easily.

In summary: here is what it means to live a life as a Vanaprastha in the Western world:

If you are equipped with an adequate philosophical background and preparation according to the true Tradition and you have gained spiritual values and maturity from the first two stages, you may begin with your systematic withdrawal. Be aware, however, that the renunciation does not arise from a mere wish to protest or to be in social opposition as a proof of your 'being different' or 'special'. Above all, this momentous step in the life of a person must come from the bottom of the heart and has to be grounded in insight and the internalization of spiritual values. Otherwise it becomes a pseudo-attitude, a wrong step without inner substance. That would rather harm you and your environment than benefit.

A person who is capable of creating a center of peace and tranquility and stillness (Asrama) in the midst of our tumultuous and hectic society, awash in excessive consumerism, and is also able to allow others to partake in this Satsanga, is truly a being whose presence a spiritual seeker should look for.

The fourth stage (Samnyasin)

The classical Indian Samnyasin (also written Sannyasin) has completely renounced the world. His lack of possessions not only refers to material poverty, but also to 'poverty of spirit' in the sense of Saint Francis and other Christian mystics. This represents highest Vairagya, which is detachment from all dualistic forms in appearance in the material, intellectual, emotional and psychological areas of life. Likes and dislikes, good and evil, God and Satan, love and hate, happiness and misery, joy and sorrow, pain and pleasure, faith in God and atheism – as pairs of opposites - all these names and forms lose their meaning.

I should like to mention here that these days there is an important indication that certain terms of the Sacred Tradition are getting misused. This indication can be found in the general moral and ethical fields and one also finds it in critical theological discussions. I deliberately won't mention specific instances of this in order not to offend anybody. However, we are looking at the serious issue of debasement of terms that carry powerful meaning and have close to mantric potency, and we find them applied in a secularized and a pseudo-spiritual manner. Even the advertising industry does not refrain from using the holiest of all mantras OM or AUM.

Raphael says that all of this is an expression of the Kali Yuga, our present Dark Age, in which the collective unconscious of global Karma, whose victims number in the billions, demotes the holy into the profane. This suggests how important it is to have Samnyasins in the world, as they operate in public or in secret on the planet by their mere presence and provide stability on spiritual levels.

In terms of our European life practice, just as with the other three stages, a life as a Samnyasin is not an unachievable utopia. The work of the total renunciate largely happens away from the public eye. He lives either in a self-sufficient way or in a community in a hermitage or in an Asrama following the order of the Tradition of the Vedas and the Upanishads. Paul Deussen (1845-1919), the great German philosopher and India expert, Sanskrit scholar, a contemporary and lifelong friend of Nietzsche, translated the sixty most important Upanishads with a quality that still sets the standards. For our theme of the four life stages one of his works is particularly interesting. From the Atharvaveda he summarized a specific collection of the Upanishads, which all deal with Samnyasa, and he published them under the name 'Samnyasa-Upanishads'. In it the life of the student is described from level one all the way to Samnyasa, who eventually renounces the world completely.

I'd like to emphasize here that this last step in a life of a seeker for God does not happen for personal gain but for the benefit of all beings.

Soham – Shanti

7. Do I Need a Teacher/ Master or Does Everything Happen by Grace?

Absorbed by the light

One morning, many years ago, I was lying on my stomach in bed when all of a sudden a small blue glow appeared in front of my inner eye. The glow grew larger and expanded more and more. It had the shape of the blue aura of a fingertip, just as one usually sees them in the Kirlian photography. High frequency, high voltage Kirlian photography can make the radiation field of a human being visible. The blurred contours of the circle of light flared like a flame. At first I hesitated to involve myself with it, but then I just let myself fall into what felt like a downwards direction, through all matter, and then it actually became a falling, which then turned into a pull, drawing me with the impression of an enormous speed through the light phenomenon into a tunnel of light.

There was a pleasant feeling of security and I had a joyful expectation of what would doubtlessly be a beautiful or at least interesting event. All at once I found myself in a house in a room with colorful walls. There were also other beings present, with whom

I communicated. Then this phenomenon or this journey faded out and I woke up in my bed with an awareness of great joy and the feeling of being guided from within.

I learned from this lesson that in transcendental events one has to trust and let go without using the mind. As soon as the Manas becomes too active, the subtle recedes again, because it belongs to a different dimension than the one we know from our physical material conditioning. Thinking as activity (Rajas Guna) is a different category of the mind than pure awareness and mindfulness, stillness-balance (Sattva Guna) or emptiness (Shunyata).

Broad studies of secret teachings

During my college years and beyond I examined and studied widely anything that had the character of a secret teaching. Esoteric, mystic, myths, parapsychology, yoga, supernatural phenomena, reincarnation and the newly established link between top-ranking sciences, mostly quantum physics and the ancient teachings of the tradition such as Taoism, Gnosis, Quaballah, Buddhism and Hinduism. The worldwide bestseller by Fritjof Capra, 'The Turning Point', and also the works of Gregory Bateson (eg. 'Steps to an Ecology of Mind') in the early of 1980s really introduced a turning point, the turning towards a new religiousness and spirituality.

Even a few years before that it had been considered impossible that there were intersections of the ancient philosophies and the most advanced contemporary scientific findings; these now became obvious, and intellectual giants such as Einstein, Niels, Bohr, Heisenberg, David Bohm, Max Planck and many others professed a humility of science in the face of God, the world and the creation. Heisenberg once described it most brilliantly:

> *'The first sip from the cup of the nature sciences makes you atheistic, but at the bottom of the cup God is waiting.'*

For me the study of all these teachings was a great and very exciting journey to the source of the Self. However, I had to content myself with the journey only. The source did not want to reveal itself. Gradually I had to accept that much knowledge still does not amount to understanding, that understanding is still not recognition and that recognition also requires a certain intuitive impulse to be realized.

Until now it had been, in the words of Vedanta, a journey from Manas to Buddhi – from purely rational, analytical gathering and knowledge to intuitively apprehending on the path of higher intellect. Ultimately, it is the turning towards renouncing of and departure from individuality and to holistic Universality. In spiritual terminology this event is known as self-realization.

But can this necessary and intuitive impulse of the Holy Fire unfold purely from studying books or from trial and error with various techniques and methods?

Let us come back to the initial question of this chapter, whether we need a teacher or a master.

Spontaneous answer: nobody needs a spiritual teacher or a master. The highest teacher is the Self. And every human being is the Self, reflected in Mahavakya Tat Tvam Asi: Thou Art That!

Does this chapter end with this well-meaning but slightly provocative argument and thus become superfluous? After all, the Tradition teaches this as its essence. For the mind, which has understood the inner core of this statement, it really is the end; it has found itself to be something higher (Buddhi). For any other individualized and ego-directed mind it is still important and highly relevant to meet a qualified teacher. Or does the liberation perhaps happen without the teacher after all, alone through the bestowing of Divine Grace?

We must state that today, in the Dark Ages, many a mind does not hesitate to give God commands such as: 'Hey, God, I have heard

I am the Supreme Self. Well then, bring it on now, this freedom, I am very probably worth it since I am equal to you. I also do not care for this preliminary stage of Saguna Brahman, that simple Samadhi, but I wish to be received right into Niguna Brahman. If it's really necessary I can also meditate a bit, but then certainly, in the foreseeable future, I expect the offer of your Grace.'

The esteemed reader may believe it or not, but such arrogance in dealing with the highest theory of knowledge does exist and the author has repeatedly encountered it in rich variations, in both public events and private meetings.

What error is happening here in such an individualized soul (Jiva)? Is it that the ego-reason-complex has sensed something, something very special? He sees a chance to present himself as somebody very special, far above the others, and to set himself in a limelight far surpassing the normal. To use the words of the Buddhist-oriented psychologist Erich Fromm, this person has landed on the 'having' side of life, even though he believes that he is reaching for the 'being' side. Fromm's concept of 'being' refers to a non-alienated existence of the human being, who is striving for self-realization.

> *'The difference between the modes of existence of 'having' and 'being' expresses itself in the field of knowing in the phraseology 'I have knowledge' and 'I know'. We can deepen our understanding of the nature of knowledge in a person who lives in the mode of 'being', when we bring to mind what thinkers like Buddha, the prophets, Jesus, Meister Eckhart, Sigmund Freud and Karl Marx had as their viewpoint. According to their perspective knowledge starts with the recognition of the deception created by the perceptions of our so-called commonsense…'*[28]

28 Fromm, Erich: Haben oder Sein ('To Have or to Be'), Stuttgart 1982, 12. Edition, page 47 f.

Fromm should be forgiven for mentioning his psychoanalyst teacher and Karl Marx in the same breath and for rolling them into one with the great mystics and founders of religions. What is important here is the core of his message. And it is consistent with the ancient traditions such as Advaita Vedanta, when he emphasizes the insight regarding the deception of the mind. Vedanta says the same about the influence of Maya on the perceiving sense organs, the ego and the mind.

In principle any amateur climber who is sufficiently trained physically can climb a mountain where the level of difficulty is not too high. Nevertheless, there are many dangers lurking there, such as the weather, geological peculiarities, animals, boulders, the risk of freezing, snow, inattentiveness and other factors, which an inexperienced person cannot know or take into consideration. He has no inkling of all their diversity and special characteristics. Therefore, the Alpine Club responsible for safety says you need a mountain guide for the Watzmann, the Zugspitze and the Matterhorn.

In the same way we can also justify the need for a spiritual teacher. The pitfalls of high mountain climbing are almost nothing compared to the very complex vortices in the human psyche. With its aspect of deception Maya holds us in such a tight grip that most people do not notice it at all, because they have been identifying with exactly that for so many lifetimes. The vast majority comes into this world with this deception. It is the legacy of the collective consciousness of humanity. So they do not even think about this deception in the course of their lives. They are not at all able to, as it is a blind spot in their individualized consciousness. I cannot deal with or change something that I am not even aware of. Only when there has been created a special attraction in former lives through contemplation, a stimulus towards transcendence of the ego-mind-complex, triggered by whatever cause, then only does a new door open for this human being in this present life. This is the door to approaching the truth of being, to the unequivocal realization of the great deception of Maya.

Right here arises the willingness to trust a teacher. With appropriate sincerity something wonderful happens: the aspirant looks for a teacher and the teacher finds the seeker. In order to illuminate this mystical process in more detail we shall use the words of some great teachers.

Sri Swami Sivananda[29] stresses emphatically the necessity for a teacher, especially for a novice on the spiritual path. To light a candle one needs an additional burning candle. So only an enlightened soul could help another to enlightenment. There are many, as the Swami says, who meditate for years and then encounter various obstacles. They soon realize that they are not able to dissolve certain (mental) blockages by themselves or to eliminate some stumbling blocks. It is in this moment at the latest that they look for a teacher. In a nice analogy Sivananda says that only the man who has already been to Badrinath can point the way there. And in the case of the spiritual search it is far more difficult to escape the subtle traps and obstacles of the mind. Rather, the mind leads us quite often into aberrations. Only the guru /teacher can always make it clear which path leads to where: into a trap or dead end or straight to liberation. Without this guidance one may think one is on the way to Badrinath, but actually finds one has come back to Delhi.

In classical Vedanta style the great Swami shows us that the nature of the ego is so strong that one cannot detect one's own weaknesses and blind spots by himself alone. Just as a man cannot see his own back he cannot recognize his own errors and mistakes. With the gracious guidance of a guru or a master and in the community of a Satsanga, centered around a qualified teacher, the aspirant

---

29 see Swami Sivananda: Bliss Divine, fifth edition 1997, Yoga Vedanta Forest Academy Press, Shivanandanagar, Himalayas, India, page 156 ff.

is optimally taken care of, in a place where he can withstand and overcome the adversities of the world. He warned about teachers who would casually say: you do not need a teacher, your Self is the teacher, you yourself are the guru etc. One should not follow such teachers, they are pseudo-gurus and not worth listening to.

To highlight the eminent importance of a guru, Swami finally points to the great avatars like Krishna, Rama and Jesus, who all had their gurus whose feet they sat at. Krishna had guru Sandeepani, Rama had guru Vasishta as a teacher and Jesus was baptized (initiated) by John.

From this we know that the need of a teacher is a Sacred Law, applicable as soon as a soul or even as a great soul enters this world. Even a direct incarnation of God abides by its own law. How presumptuous can an ego-directed soul be to assume that it can make God Himself his guru without the intermission of a physical guru. Sivananda agrees and says that it might be possible, but then this soul must have certain qualifications such as Manas polished clean as a mirror, ethical perfection and must come equipped with powerful virtues. And then additionally it needs to be far beyond body consciousness and then it could perhaps relinquish the need for the guru, the divinely incarnated soul. We should add that by Grace this happens to perhaps one in a million people. And it can happen only because of karmically accumulated merits from previous existences.

In addition to his criticism regarding the pseudo-gurus Swami Sivananda points to the recommended alternatives for those not able to find a highly realized guru, whom he calls first-class-guru. In this case one can then just entrust oneself to a teacher who has been on the path of the highest knowledge for many years, preferably one who has himself been initiated by a Master and who possesses the required qualities. These are purity of mind and other great virtues and disposition of deep knowledge and understanding of the scriptures.

Should it not be possible for someone to even find a teacher of the second kind, he is then referred to the authentic scriptures of the enlightened masters like Vyasa, Shankara or Dattatreya. If these masters were dearly revered and their writings were thoroughly studied, and if one would meditate regularly, then at the right time when the soul is mature the highest Lord would ensure a meeting between a teacher and a disciple in a divinely mystical manner.

The great Bhakta Sri Ramakrishna[30] liked to enchant his listeners with examples from nature. He describes some experiences of a sage who saw symbols that are typical of a guru in the behavior of animals. Here is an example:

> *The sage found another guru in a bee. The bee had gathered honey with great effort over many months when somebody came, broke open the beehive and took the honey. The bee was not destined to reap the fruits of her cumbersome labor. When the sage saw this he bowed to the bee saying: 'Revered one, you are my guru. I have learned from you what is the sure fate of accumulated wealth.'*

Then Ramakrishna gives us a very unusual hint from the viewpoint of the teacher:

> *There are hundreds of teachers…, but it is difficult to find a single disciple. Many can give good advice, but few are willing to follow it.*

30 Sri Ramakrishna: Worte des Meisters ('Words of the Master'), Rascher Verlag, Zuerich 1949, s. page 23 ff.

And he also classifies teachers and names their characteristics with clarity and strictness:

> *The guru who gives instructions to his disciple to do religious exercises without worrying about if they are followed or not is a third-class guru. The second-class guru explains the rules to his students, he repeats the explanations until they are understood correctly and he makes sure that his instructions are followed. The first-class guru is not content with giving instructions and making sure that they are followed. He will, if necessary, force upon the disciple the initially bitter medicine of strenuous spiritual exercises.*

Swami Vivekananda was the most famous disciple of Sri Ramakrishna, and was also the most important and the most formidable in using language. Let us also listen to him as he makes some additions.[31] Similar to Shivananda he also emphasizes that a soul can only receive impulses from another soul. The study of books, even of the most sacred ones, initially only stokes the intellect and does not lead to any spiritual progress. A highly developed intellect does not necessarily go hand in hand with or is directly proportional to a higher spiritual development, as many mistakenly believe. Only in the spiritual life practice is it possible to determine if someone has made spiritual progress.

So it depends on the implementation of spiritual instructions. He expresses the dual qualities in simple, but very clear words:

> *The one who speaks of religion has to be beautiful,…and equally so the soul that receives the impulse, … and when both are beautiful and extraordinary, then the most marvelous*

31 Swami Budhananda (publisher): Teachings of Swami Vivekananda. 5. Edition, 1971, Calcutta

spiritual growth happens, and otherwise not. These are the real teachers and these are the real disciples.

Answering the question about how to know a teacher, Vivekananda says, the sun requires no torch to make it visible. When the sun rises we know it immediately and when the teacher of men comes to help us then the soul knows intuitively that Truth has already begun to shine upon him. In regard to the teacher we must see that he knows the hidden meaning of the scriptures. In his typically flippant and critical, but very sharp-witted style, Vivekananda refers to the Holy Scriptures as 'the dry bones of religion'. With that statement he is not devaluing the scriptures but indicating that their concealed content can only be brought into the light of consciousness with the help of a qualified teacher. He sees the teacher as the bearer of spiritual power. And this happens only through the medium of (impersonal, divine) love. Considering this the teacher has only one task: to be the 'eye-opener of religion'.

At the conclusion of his remarks on the importance of the teacher, Vivekananda admonishes us in his vivid language that we may search for Truth in the Himalayas or in the Alps, in the Caucasus or in the deserts Gobi and Sahara, or even at the bottom of the sea, but the unveiling of religion will only come when we find a teacher. We should then serve him with childlike innocence, freely open our hearts to his influence and see God manifested in him. There is nothing more magnificent and sacred than the pure knowledge that is transmitted to a soul by a teacher.

Nisargadatta Maharaj[32] and Ramana Maharshi[33] throw the questioner who asks about the significance of the guru always back to

---

32 Ramesh S. Balsekar: Pointers from Nisargadatta Maharaj, Chetana Ltd. 2 Edition, 1999, Kalaghoda, Mumbai, India , p. 67 ff.

33 Ramana Maharshi: Talks with the Sage from Arunachala, Ansata Verlag, Zuerich 1989, cf. p. 13, 30, 158 ff.

himself: Find the one who is asking or ask yourself: 'Who am I?' This way of questioning (self-enquiry) dissolves all thoughts and ultimately even the ego.

The teacher shows the way to action without expectation (Karma Yoga). The sage asked a scholar from the Sorbonne if he had already intended to visit Ramana while still in Paris. The scholar said no. And so in this case the master attests that this is unintentional action. According to the Gita the purpose of our birth (Dharma) must be fulfilled whether we like it or not. Therefore it would be best to allow life itself to decide how it should unfold. We should allow the purpose to fulfill itself.

Well, we know how hard it is to follow this advice. Who can switch off his mind in everyday life or while making plans leave everything to his Dharma. Nevertheless, that is exactly what it is about: follow the instructions of the Vedanta teacher, hand your life over to God and live by the word from the Bible 'Thy will be done'. In Ramana's subtle words:

> *The cosmic mind, which becomes manifest in a few very rare beings, has the power to connect in others the individual (weak) mind with the Universal (strong) mind of inner depth. Such a rare being is called a guru and he is the Divine become manifest.*

The master of Ramesh Balsekar, Nisargadatta Maharaj, sums up the outstanding qualities of a teacher/master and what he is in the finest Advaita Philosophia. This is totally different from his disciple, who has drifted off course and has become fatalistic. We shall render the text, translated from English by the author, in a greatly summarized version:

The calamity arises because man looks upon himself as an individual, as individualized entity. And that is also how he sees the guru, just as another individualized entity who somehow appears to be different in brain and heart, which makes him an enlightened person, however merely a different kind of person. And exactly here is the big mistake. The guru has realized, in whatever way, that he is the Ultimate Reality; he looks upon each living being without distinction as upon himself, but never as a person or some kind of thing or form.[34]

Nisargadatta speaks to us, almost as a consolation and hope, even as a kind of formula for success:

The faster the identification with the body as a separate entity can be dropped the faster the Grace of the guru will flourish in the consciousness of the disciple.[35]

Once, when I asked my revered Master Raphael[36] in the 1990s about initiations in the classical Vedanta Tradition, he looked at me intently and said, that each Darshan with Raphael and with one of his acknowledged disciples is an initiation. In the mystery schools of the western Tradition around Pythagoras, Parmenides, Plato, Plotinus and other wise philosophers of those times it was a great exception to be accepted as a disciple because of the high standards and therefore only few qualified. This is still the case today in the traditions that like Advaita Vedanta initiate. That is why a master usually has only a very few disciples.

---

34 ibidem, loc. cit. p. 70

35 ibid loc. cit. p. 70

36 Author's note: Raphael mostly uses the third person when he talks about himself. Where there is no Ego the first person grammatically is also missing.

We want to conclude this chapter with some urgent messages:

Yes, the earnest seeker of truth needs a teacher, because a soul that is not well prepared has virtually no chance to escape the prison of individuality and separation from the Divine and the world as such due to Maya with its two main elements of deception and projection. Life after life we are born into the sometimes sweet, sometimes cruel domination by Maya and we spend our lives in the physical universe in a huge variety of conditions on this or some other planet. However, mostly we live in sorrowful ignorance (Avidya) in the form of pleasure-pain, joy-sorrow, euphoria-depression, lethargy-action and more of the same. We are victims of our six senses[37] within duality, which we consider to be a given and therefore true.

For eons we have been friendly and tightly bound to our physical externality, within a universe that exists only externally. Granted, not everything of the inner is denied, because we do feel and experience this aspect. But the medical and neural sciences want to hammer into us that all these perceptions are just fantasies and constructs of our brain, and therefore imaginations, fictions, assumptions and non-realities, because realities are 'tangible' only on the outside.

And then 98 percent of all the relevant nature scientists bow out when it involves inner spiritual notions as in religion, which are even beyond the power of imagination. Since the appearance of quantum knowledge physicists have shown themselves to be much more open-minded and mature, more holistic in their thinking than the majority of modern medical doctors.

Many products and services from the current electronic communication playground are pure seductions of Maya. Why? They completely captivate the already materialistic human mind in such a way

37 Thinking, in Vedanta the ability to think is considered to be the sixth sense.

that it hardly looks at itself any more, as in attempting to find out its own original unconditioned state.

In earlier days, especially during the Middle Ages because of the tremendous physical drudgery and the rampant epidemics, people hardly had any time to devote to focused religious enquiry. Today the technical temptations and material prosperity of the Western world are the reasons for the forgetting of the Self. Therefore in every epoch we need sublime beings who can help us escape from the mousetrap. The ancient Traditions have promised us that in every age these helping beings will incarnate on earth, partly recognized, partly in secret, but always helpful. They exist on different planes of existence, in the gross physical as well as in the spiritual, in heaven and on earth.

The task for us normal earthlings is to rediscover our true Dharma, to follow the subtle call of the soul, to meet a worthy teacher/master and to take the bold leap into the void full of infinite fullness.

Oh brother, oh sister,

Start right NOW with that!

OM – Shanti

8. Why Classical Advaita Vedanta Instead of Fast-Track Salvation?

Eating, drinking, sleeping! A little laughter; much pain and weeping. Is this really all to life? Do not die here like an earthworm. Wake up, finally, and attain immortal Bliss.

Swami Sivananda shouts his simple and timeless message with such intensity to us. It is quite astonishing how much our innermost being is obscured by the veils of Avidya. This makes us cope with our daily lives as if we were programmed robots, without the slightest reflection of a mature mind upon the light behind these disguises.

In the first chapter we have looked a little bit at the historical roots of Advaita Vedanta and have wondered how is it that such an old teaching still has the power to exist in our modern world and to give hope to people. At the time of Adi Shankara the world was quite different than it is today, and it was all the more so 6,000 years ago, the time when the oral transmission of the Vedas began. When the wise ancients created these wonderful philosophies there was one question they really did not have to worry about: is the teaching going to be valid in a few hundred years time? The initiating teaching of Advaita is pure metaphysics, pure Philosophia Perennis. It is the written reflection of the One Eternal Truth, Sanatana Dharma, always valid, an imperishable property of humanity, a gift of God through the mouths and hands of His great manifestations on earth.

They are all-encompassing explanations of man and the world from the internal structure of human nature to the Cosmos in the form of gross and subtle universes. This is not mental knowledge that has been written down, but it is the direct vision of Truth, which pours its everlasting radiance and dignity upon us ignorants as sutras in a word-language composed by masters.

In our time one finds numerous attempts by modern eloquent teachers to try to 'break down' this enormous heritage to the level of a child just starting school. They want to show how simple the Truth is and how easy it is to obtain it. It is a cute attempt to try to appeal to the masses, which respond well to simplicity. Quite a few of them would find it far more attractive and interesting to achieve this important goal without much effort than to win big in lottery. After all, with this one promises to have lasting happiness.

We could compare this with a normal intelligent ten-year-old boy, who goes to a math teacher and demands that he please just quickly teach him calculus, so that he could calculate the winding, irregular surface of a natural lake. What can the experienced and well-meaning teacher, who welcomes and appreciates the motivation of the young student, do in such a case but set boundaries? He advises the young man to, in the next four to six years, deepen his basic arithmetic operations, to learn quadratic equations, algebra, differential calculus and vector analysis etc. Then he would be ready to present his request again.

In the past but also these days, a Zen roshi sends his disciple to sit in Zazen until he has non-rationally solved his paradoxical koan. Jesus referred to the pure love of the Lord. Buddha pointed to the way as the goal. Ramakrishna requested unconditional devotion to God and to the Divine Mother. Shankara established the six main characteristics of a disciple as a strategy for liberation of the Jnana Yogi. Patanjali formed the finely structured eightfold path of Ashtanga Yoga as part of the Yoga Sutra. Raphael teaches the Oneness of the Eastern and Western One Tradition in all its complex structures. Sri Aurobindo left behind the comprehensive Integral Yoga. Sri Yukteswarji adopted into words and lived the Holy Science, and his popular disciple Paramahansa Yogananda, following the instructions of his master, created Krya Yoga for the West. This list could go on.

What do the lives and works of these great souls teach us? They all have a common core. And that core is not just alike but really the same: they all refer to the eternal Truth of the Holy Shruti as it was set down in writing. None of them has ever said that the way back to the Self would be easy. Indeed, it is said the Truth is simple, but this may not be interpreted as meaning that anybody can grab hold of it in the twinkling of an eye. Only one who does his homework sincerely and who develops the deep understanding and also the courage to work on the irrevocable surmounting of the ego and the Manas can attain it. No matter what name one calls it, this is the only path to salvation without return, the path without the possibility of returning to individuality.

Now we slowly begin to understand why it is not possible to radically trim down the One Tradition and remain unpunished.[38] If Brahma-Atman-Isvara had wanted to reduce the Tradition down to one aspect, to the message: 'You already are enlightened, there

---

38 Please understand that punishment is not the wrath of God as such, but a self-induced karmic consequence of ignorance.

is nothing to gain, you cannot do anything', then the Shruti would have consisted of a three-liner rather than of thousands of pages. And then humanity would be in the iron grip of an absolute fatalism, against which even a politically imposed system of determinism would look like a paradise, no matter in which era it would occurre.

One thing, however, should be said in favor of the great simplifiers: when the simplicity of their message strikes a mature soul that has been living life relatively unaware of his potential, there is a possibility under specific circumstances that a wave is initiated which could carry that soul to the goal of liberation. However, that would be only possible if a teacher is involved who himself has already merged with the ocean and is not just standing on the shore preaching. But for all other souls who have not come that close to the Truth such pronouncements are nothing but sound and smoke and before long are scattered in the winds of the cosmic atmosphere.

On close inspection one sees that in this world of becoming (Samsara) from birth, life and death everything happens in a leisurely manner. The laws of nature here on earth are in no hurry! Life and learning are successive processes that happen step by step, going forwards, backwards or are even stagnating. In such a lethargic sort of world (Tamas Guna) how could the subtle spiritual unfolding of man happen in leaps of all things, as an emergence?[39] And in addition to all this we are in the Dark Age in which everything spiritual is pulled down into the profane. The sacred becomes the profane. From the point of view of religious studies the renowned researcher Mircea Eliade[40] describes the ambivalence of our zeitgeist in this way:

---

39 Emergence is a leap in biological and mental evolution, which up to now has not been explained on the rational-scientific level.

40 Mircea Eliade: Das Heilige und das Profane, (The Sacred and the Profane), Insel Verlag, Frankfurt am Main, 1984, p. 175

'By re-actualizing sacred history, by imitating the Divine behavior, man puts and keeps himself close to the gods, that is, into the Real and Meaningful.

It is easy to see all that separates this mode of being in the world from the existence of non-religious man. First of all, the non-religious man refuses transcendence, he accepts the relativity of the 'reality', and may even come to doubt the meaning of existence... In the modern societies of the West the non-religious man has developed fully...he assumes a new existential situation; he regards himself solely as the subject and agent of history and he refuses all appeal to Transcendence...Man > makes himself<, and he can only make himself completely in proportion to how much he desacralizes himself and the world.'

Eliade reveals here a very terrible and very sad realization: man in Kali Yuga has removed himself extremely far from the Divine and is very busy creating his relative world in such a way that he believes it to be absolute. A world without purpose, without hope, without stability, without meaning. An existence that is a type of vegetating during a lifetime, sometimes nice, sometimes terrible and which sinks into a dark nothingness with death. All of this reminds us strongly of the nihilism of Nietzsche. He has, however, remained unrecognized as a warning prophet of modernity or has been misunderstood.

Classical Advaita Vedanta not only gives courage to man but it also leads directly to the bliss of the Self. It takes into account the extraordinary complexity of the human-divine nature and leads gently but unmistakably and clearly from one level of insight to the next higher one until the ultimate goal – Moksha, the liberation – is not only reached, but fully realized. We learn more about the structure of ourselves as beings, about the gross and subtle cosmos with all its beings and planes of existence. We can recognize while alive the certainty of survival after death. If parents could provide their children with such high intellectual and spiritual knowledge instead of preparing them for an increasingly decadent world then this would be the most valuable gift that a father or a mother can give to them.

Raphael reminds us in his writings again and again that this world can not be saved via social, altruistic or political programs, no matter how well intended they might be. Only a consciousness that has risen to the transcendental can change the world.[41]

> *'A mechanistic historical philosophy of becoming inevitably results in nullity and traumatic nihilism…*
>
> *The philosophy of becoming is a philosophy of physical needs. But the being consists of more than excrement and sperm, it also has an intellect (noûs)[42]. To forget that means to not recognize the most important and essential part.*
>
> *The being is infinite and universal, and only through the transcending of his physical prison can he find full freedom and fulfillment. Any other freedom is illusory, a false freedom.'*[43]

In the classical Advaita Vedanta of Shankara the transcendence of the ego-Manas complex is one of the first major goals. It is already such a high goal that it is usually greatly underestimated in its importance and difficulty to realize. It is so to speak the Moksha -1-stage, the first great liberation. The ego and the Manas are dissolved and integrated into the Buddhi. The person dissolves with it. Man depersonalizes and becomes a being that beholds, or to be

---

41 compare e.g. Raphael: Welche Demokratie? (Which Democracy?) Pointers for a good government, Regin Verlag, Straelen, 2006

42 Here Raphael does not mean the Manas-intellect, but the higher intellect, the Buddhi, the Universal View.

43 ibid loc. cit. page 136

more precise, that 'recognizes' life, human beings, nature, the animals, God and the Cosmos as One in Universal View. This tremendous step in the existence of a human being is normally referred to as enlightenment. But it is by no means the last stage of the ascending soul. There are still many steps up to the integral One Isvara, to Maha-Atma, first manifestation of the creation in Saguna Brahman, the great Universal Soul, and ultimately to the One without the second, Brahman-Atman or Nirguna Brahman; this is Brahman without attributes.

At this point a well-intended critical word to all friends of the quick-and-easy or instant self-realization is needed: those who think that their small belief in the existence of a deity will be enough to free them as quickly as possible from the yoke of physicality if they just ask and pray sufficiently, they are truly very naïve. And those who believe some proclaimers of alleged truth that promise superfast realization and quick and simplified salvation have our sympathy and compassion because they do not intelligently utilize their ability for discrimination (Viveka), which God has endowed them with.

Let's repeat it: In the significantly slowed-down world of becoming 99.99% of human beings cannot make spiritual 'kangaroo' super-jumps without falling and injuring themselves. Therefore they should learn to accept the offer of Shruti and Smirti[44] that has been blessed with Divine love and to utilize the sophistication, wealth and clarity of the One Tradition. First with the intellect and then after some progress by opening the heart (Anahata-Chakra) and receiving the divine inspirations without any effort.

Also, be careful with the easy and wonderful promises associated with enlightenment or the experience of cosmic consciousness through the power of Kundalini energy. In his work as a psycho-

44 Shruti, the non-human Tradition; Smirti, scriptures from the sages and the wise.

therapist the author has met quite a few pitiful beings who have used techniques - in spite of their unprepared overall situation – leading to Chakras being energetically ripped open and the resulting liberation of sleeping Kundalini leading to psychotic conditions. Anyone who does such a thing is a criminal, more so than somebody who robs a store. He destroys a human life, often irreversibly. On both sides, the one who caused the damage and the victim, there arise enormous karmic entanglements and energies, which can be carried over into another existence, into a new incarnation.

Many of the surprisingly violent psychological disorders in our societies do not originate from childhood or later years in an adult life, but have been carried over from one or several earlier lives. And it is not infrequent that one re-encounters exactly the same entities with whom this karma has been established. Fateful entanglement. New opportunities, but also new risks, immediately come to life. Karma cannot only be removed but may, on the contrary, also increase.

Blessed is he who is equipped with sufficient Viveka and Vairagya[45] to be able to free himself from the stranglehold of karmic burdens, to dissolve the old karma. Blessed is he who has found a spiritual teacher who is genuine and authentic and who can show him the way out of the maze. Blessed is he who has become spiritually rooted in the Sacred Tradition and who does not receive his power from a fitness center but who bathes in the living flow of divine Prana, drinks from it and soothes his soul.

In his hermitage many years ago Raphael explained to me the real and powerful side, or perhaps the benefits, if you will, of engagement with the scriptures of Shruti and Smirti:

---

45 Viveka, higher discrimination ability of the intellect (noûs), not analytical thinking; Vairagya, here to be understood as detachment, distance, renunciation and non-attachment.

'As soon as you read the scriptures with an open heart, with care and attentiveness, a spiritual wave rises from your being, which becomes visible in the mental world[46] and immediately flows back as blissful power into your being and purifies and calms the mind.'

Dear reader! As a classical Vedanta teacher I tune into the canon of the modern proclaimers of instant enlightenment in my own way: yes, it is very easy to find the Truth, you just have to:

- Be ready for it
- Commit to a teaching that initiates you
- Find a qualified and authentic guru
- Study the scriptures with a wide-open heart (Anahata Chakra) and contemplate on them
- Align your life towards the Sacred instead of the profane
- Join a Satsang that is conducted in a qualified way
- Establish disciple qualifications, primarily Viveka and Vairagya, based on an unquenchable thirst for the Truth, and finally
- Embed your life in modesty, simplicity, humility and devotion to the Divine (Isvara)

If you can fulfill these, the main criteria of a true disciple, then the Truth comes to you by itself, it reveals itself totally naturally. Then you are truly a blessed being whose mere presence can already help other people towards a spiritual breakthrough.

46 Manavaloka, the third level above the physical and astral light-world. Here is the center of the reason (mind), a universe of mental power, which every human being owns; most people believe that the mind is located in the brain and is even its product, as the medical sciences want us to believe.

With all it takes, fulfill these requirements as well as you can, and start a new life practice. Recognize yourself as the Self and you are forever free.

Dattatreya, the great Avatara world teacher, the true Jagad guru, embodiment of the living teaching, calls to us in the Avadhuta Gita, chapter 1, Verses 13-15:

You are not born,
nor do you die.
At no time do you have a body.
It is well-known:
'All is Brahman.'

You are He who is exterior and interior.
You are the auspicious One
existing everywhere at all times.
Why is it that you are deluded,
And why are you running hither and thither
like a ghost?

Union and separation
exist in regard neither to you nor to me.
There is no you,
no me,
nor is there this universe.
All is verily
the Self alone.

Contemplate these verses whether you are advanced or beginner, and the spiritual wave will rise.

May there be Blessings.

Shanti.

9. Prisoner of the Kali Yuga – or Is There a Way Out?

A Sannyasin was sitting under a huge banyan tree about to meditate, when along came a well-known holy man. The Sannyasin seized the opportunity to ask him something that had been on his mind for a long time: Oh Master, how many lives do I have to spend on earth until enlightenment? The holy man answered: look at the crown of this banyan tree under which you sit. The number of its leaves corresponds to the number of your impending lives. The seeker in this ancient Indian story exclaimed, overjoyed: Oh Lord, only that number of lives?

The response of a Western person would have certainly been quite different: would have been accompanied by a cry of horror. Here we are looking at culture-specific values, which in India are very different from those of the Western world, particularly in the area of religion.

We humans live on a time axis. The perception of time depends on different parameters such as attentiveness, engagement, distraction, concentration etc. If somebody is too late for an appointment, for example a date with a new love, each minute of delay feels like an eternity. If someone reads a book with fascination or watches an interesting movie or is very busy, time goes by very quickly. Time is therefore a relative factor with different associated feelings, depending on the nature of the consciousness. In the rich treasure of Indian parables there is an example of the snake and the frog.

> A snake has a frog in its mouth. Only the head of the frog still looks out. Within a few moments it will be completely devoured. But the poor frog still quickly shoots out his tongue to catch some insects.

Man engulfed in ignorance lives just like that. We are already in the all-devouring mouth of Kala[47], time; in a just few moments, oh Man, you will disappear into nowhere. And still you hold on to sense objects incessantly. You have become a victim and a slave of a great illusion, delusion, deception and attachment (Moha). The ordinary man has no idea of the importance of time.

Time is more valuable than money, more valuable than anything else of value in the world. Time is the most precious treasure we have. In the Indian spiritual view time is considered as 'the soul of the world' or 'time is life'. That is why it is necessary for the seeker to use time wisely for spiritual aspiration. Only the wise men, the true seers and saints, who have realized God have escaped from time, which otherwise has unlimited power. Only the Divine Eternal is without time. For the Advaitin this means: Brahman transcends all time, Brahman is eternal, without beginning, without end, without birth, without becoming and demise. It is the timeless single One Reality.

This discourse about time leads us seamlessly to contemplation of our contemporary time, which as we already know, is considered to be the Dark Ages. For a better understanding we allow ourselves

---

47 Kala characterizes time as well as death or the God Yama, the Lord of death. All three factors are related in the life of a human being.

a glimpse into a special section of the Tradition, which can give us a clearer insight into Suchness, the modalities of our time in the 21st Century.

The Puranas[48] speak of four great ages, the Yugas:

1. Krita or Satya Yuga
2. Treta Yuga
3. Dvapara Yuga
4. The contemporary Kali Yuga

The numerical classification of these world ages is perhaps better presented in a chart for an easier understanding:

Age /Yuga	Length Human years	Length God years	Brief Description
Krita/Satya Yuga	1.728.000	4.800	The ideal or golden age
Treta Yuga	1.296.000	3.600	Integrity decreases by 25%
Dvapara Yuga	864.000	2.400	Only sparse seeking for Truth
Kali Yuga	432.000	1.200	Falling asleep spiritually
Sum of the ages = one Maha Yuga, one great world age	4.320.000	12.000	2.000 of these Maha Yugas (Kalpa) compare to one day-and-night cycle of Brahma, the creator God of the trinity

48 The Puranas are 18 main texts of the Holy Scriptures, which belong to a specific style of Hindu literature. These are not heroic epics as we know them in the West, but the focus is the workings of Isvara and the love for him (Bhakti). These are Holy Scriptures, not mere stories. These are attributed to Avatar 'Veda-Vyasa' (et al) who is also supposed to have written the Mahabharata and the Brahma-Sutra.

Let us conclude the understanding of the world ages with another short calculation:

> 12,000 God years make a Katur-or Maha Yuga.
>
> 71 of these Maha Yugas are called a Manvantara, including their two-part God-day/night-periods.
>
> 14 of these Mahavantaras make a Kalpa of 4,320,000,000 – in words: four billion, three hundred and twenty million years.

Interestingly, this number corresponds somewhat to the contemporary estimated age of our earth. We cannot give any comment about this in this book. The reader may form his own opinion. What is interesting, however, is that there are similar perceptions in scientific areas and religious traditions.

For illustration, or perhaps utter confusion, we should like to mention these gigantic time periods briefly: one such Kalpa of 4.3 billion years corresponds to one *night (!)* in Brahma's life. And Brahma lives *100 years (!)*.

For the sake of the probity of religious sciences it should be noted that there is yet another view in regard to these calculations. And that is the calculation of the great sage Sri Yukteswar (1855 – 1936), the Master of Paramahansa Yogananda. He writes in his book 'The Sacred Science', that this old way of calculating is based on mistakes of the Rishis, who lived in some Kali Yuga, a Dark Age, and therefore did not understand the ancient traditions any more. Yukteswar's methodology of calculation is based on astrological cycles. Thus, the Yugas are respectively shorter.

But what difference does a few million years more or less make for us mere mortals? What is important is the dominant world vibration of the time. Let us summarize the characteristics of the four Yugas once more in order to have a closer look at our current age and to ask ourselves if we are in fact subject to the fatal modus of our age-destiny or if there is a way out from the 'hell of Kali Yuga'.

Krita or Satya Yuga

The four ages inter alia are described in the Manu-Samhita, the book of laws of Manu[49]. Krita Yuga is considered as a time in which the connection to the gods (in Advaita understood as beings in the Brahmaloka who support mankind) was still intact and direct. Therefore it is also called the Golden Age. Hatred, grief, sorrow, jealousy, anger, selfishness, aggression or threat did not exist. Everything was simple: one God, one Veda, one rite, one law, selflessness, righteousness and dutiful implementation of the divine law was the norm. It was a life without separation between man and God, inside and outside, good and evil. The word 'Satya' contains 'Guna Sattva'. It is the Guna of Universality, safe balancing of the lower Gunas and the acquisition of the One View of world, God and life.

Treta Yuga

This is the beginning of the gradual dimming of the world. Instead of the direct contact with the gods and the predominant consciousness of Oneness, the performance of sacrificial rituals and ceremonies becomes practiced by preference. The separation from the divine has begun through a process of individualization. The righteousness of the beings decreases by one quarter. Declining respectability, reliability, incorruptibility and decency are the consequences. A bitter foretaste of our world of today is felt. Reward and punishment are the new principles of dealing with each other. The sense of duty towards God and humans has decreased.

---

49 Manu or the Manus according to the Vedas represent the first divine lawgivers and are seen as mediators between the humans and the divine. They established the sacrificial rituals and ceremonies for worship of God. 14 Manus are mentioned. In the current age the seventh Manu called (Viavasvata) rules in the ethereal realms for protection and as the regulatory authority of mankind.

Dvapara Yuga

Righteousness has now shrunk by a dynamically linear 50%. Meanwhile there are four Vedas (the ones we know) instead of the one Veda. Only members of the relevant social class study them. Up to this day in India this is the Brahmans. People understand what is revealed in them, however, to understand immediately beyond the Manas, in terms of the higher intellect (Buddhi) can be accomplished by only a few. A Pandit might be able to recite all the scriptures by heart, but the true content, the core meaning and the divine vibration of Brahama-Atman, which is hidden in it is unfortunately not comprehensible to the person who is merely 'learned'. That is the case in every religion.

Kali Yuga

The attentive reader may now ask what else can come in Kali Yuga, what kind of escalation into the bottomless evil, the impurity and separation is still possible. Actually, it is superfluous to say something in regard to this. One only has to attentively observe life today.

According to Tradition in the Dark Ages only a weak quarter of the original righteousness remains. The spiritual aspect of the human life undergoes a comatose shock. Nobody is seriously interested in spiritual practice(s) (!). Higher knowledge falls into oblivion and becomes, at best, legends that are not taken seriously, that are thought unrealistic pipe dreams.

Duality and separation from the divine principle flourish. The world however experiences this duality in a rather one-sided fashion, leaning towards evil. Do not worry, dear reader, the evil is not more powerful than the good, but it is craftier, faster, cunning and sneaky. The deception business of Maya is well underway at full speed. In the last countdown of the fading Maha Yuga man is being tested to the limits of his physical, mental, and psychological capacities. Most people are left behind because they cannot make the jump into the Universal due to becoming too deeply involved and too intensely engaged with the world. They are attached to matter, power, fame and superficial prosperity. They do not see through the transience of earthly happiness. Only a shock delivered through suffering or an encounter with a holy being can jolt them into wakefulness. All the great savior souls have appeared in succession in this age, which began in 3102 BC: Rama, Krishna, Buddha, Lao Tzu, Plato, Christ, Shankara and many other wise and God-realized beings, up to the present time.

It is a Divine promise that Divine Avatars and most exquisite Messiahs will come to help put the world in order again and again, so that the power of Divine Dharma continues to be available to human beings in their tragic oblivion after the fall of the soul, especially in times dominated by disease, exhaustion, hunger, anger, fear, despair and crime.

With regard to the initial question at the beginning of this chapter, we can say: yes, definitely there is hope for salvation. Even in the Kali Yuga we can get in touch again with the Divine principle of Isvara and even with the One without the second, Brahma. To be more exact: we can re-discover ourselves as THAT which we ARE. Brahman.

'Know thyself (as your Self)', the oracle of Delphi has called to us for thousands of years.

But are we able to do it? Good question!

Reading books and making affirmative suggestions such as: I am Brahman, then let's do it! – will not work at all. It will also not do to chant the mantra Om a hundred thousand times, if the heart is not open and involved. Even the sincerely pre-set defaults of

Manas – using cognitive concepts to understand the world and God – will not lead to success. If that were the case then all people with an intelligence quotient above 100 would immediately enter into Nirguna Brahman.

Descartes said: I think therefore I am. Advaita says: You think therefore you are not. Is this an irresolvable conflict? Not at all. These two statements are not the same consideration merely looked at from different standpoints. It is simply a Cartesian error. What Descartes overlooked or did not realize was the following: through the perception of thinking the being thinks that it exists. After all, the being has consciousness and knows that it exists because it can think. So far so good. The Manas (the thinker), however, cannot perceive himself and has no idea that he is being watched by the witness. Behind the thinker is the witness (Atman). Only the witness knows that the huge deception in the perception of existence of man is exactly this act of thinking.

Vedanta teaches us insistently: as long as you think, you are in Avidya, ignorance, non-being, unreality. Therefore, from this higher viewpoint this applies: you think therefore you are not.

Stop thinking

And get anchored in being.

That is the clear message of Advaita Vedanta.

Another aspect: as long as we think, we are in individuality. Only in the silence of no-thought do we experience being, and that's when the Buddhi takes over supremacy in its Oneness-View and Universality. The Buddhi dissolves the ego and the Manas through integration into the Transcendence of Universal Divinity.

The general recommendation for an effective escape from Kali Yuga is recognition and not thinking. Thinking happens with the psychological instrument Manas in cooperation with the ego. It is a true 'love affair' between the two. Co-dependant. Recognition cannot be acquired, it just happens. How? Through systematic preparation of Jivatman, due to favorable karmic circumstances, the thirst for truth and loving guidance by a guru, master, teacher. He guides the being in the right direction both internally and externally.

Which direction?

Now I will tell you something, dear friend - man and woman - that you perhaps have not expected:

It guides you back in the direction of Satya Yuga! Yes, you have read correctly: Satya Yuga. What many seekers and some teachers as well may not know is that while we live collectively in the Kali Yuga each individual being has the opportunity to leave the Kali Yuga through spiritual growth and qualification, to annul it in his personal existence and to create conditions that let him appear as a materialized part of the collective in the Dark Ages while his state of consciousness already exists somewhere completely different. Christian terminology would put it thus: he is in heaven, while he is walking on the earth.

That is the authentic liberation from Kali Yuga.

May this liberation happen

For all sincere souls,

May they rise into the Universal

And be light beings

Showing the way into the light

And the limitless freedom

To those humans engulfed in darkness.

May the Grace of Maha-Atma

The Universal Soul, Isvara,

Bring this about.

OM Shanti.

10. Individuality and Universality – Contradiction?

After the last wish
of the individual mind
infinity and
unconditional freedom
illuminates in brilliant radiance

Elios –

Unusual Help

On a beautiful sunny day in mid-summer, just before the turn of the millennium I was gripped by the idea that I had to get my son's 50cc scooter moving again, at least a little, to make sure it stayed mobile. Only a couple times up and down the street and it's done.

No sooner said than done, but I thought maybe I should go just a little further down the hill. Since I had planned on only a short drive outside the front door, I wasn't wearing a helmet or any protective clothing, but had on airy, summery shorts and short sleeves. Then, on the slightly sloping road I came across a tapered left turn with loose gravel in the road, and slipped out hard, the scooter flying from under me. I hit the street and slid a few meters through the gravel. I was pretty badly injured on the left side of the body, the skin deeply scraped by the fine stones, and I could barely move my left arm.

In short, I was taken to an emergency clinic, x-rayed and doctored, and despite the x-ray, they overlooked a partial dislocation (subluxation, partial dislocation of the shoulder joint) and nonetheless recommended an operation. I asked for time to think about it and would let them know because I wasn't spontaneously prepared to undergo an operation.

So I spent a few days at home and had some incredible pain. One night I was still sitting in the room wracked with pain when suddenly I heard distinct, clear internal instructions: "Stand up and go to the mirror." Then came instructions for making some very fine movements and postures. There were no words, but something happened that I just had to allow, without my own thinking. I just simply watched my body movements in the mirror. Within a few minutes it made a quick tug and a crack, and my shoulder joint was put right again. I was immediately able to move my arm again in all directions without pain, was able to sleep again, and quickly recovered from the accident.

Vedanta teaches us that once we have reached a certain level of earnestness, dignity, humility and maturity in the quest for liberation, we are never again alone. We then enjoy the protection of the gods, the beings of the Brahmaloka, a high level world in the Universal. These are not fictions, placebos, imaginations or hallucinations. These are real entities who work from a real plane of existence with us and for us.

With the blessing of the gods our delicate spiritual young 'soul-tree' grows and matures to a huge tree of life, which can withstand all shocks. It has its roots in the ground and its crown in the heavens. The connection to the gods is made.

Individuality and Universality are no contradiction, because the individual is contained in the Universal. The unity in Universal Being also includes the non-existence of individuality. The latter dissolves in it like a drop in the ocean.

When Vedanta speaks of the "Universal" it refers to the whole of creation, expressed in multiplicity. In Vedantic terminology: the Isvara-Principle, the personal God. The multiplicity of worlds and their beings is unlimited, but not absolute. If it were absolute, then all created things would recreate themselves independently, would require no causality, and all beings would be bound forever to the multiplicity. Freedom, liberation and redemption would be pure fiction.

On the other hand, when considering the human being, the concept of the Universal is separate from the individual. While the individual is represented by its three states of consciousness (waking, dreaming and deep sleep) and the limiting ego-sense (Ahankara), in a transition to the Universal a huge window opens that dissolves and integrates the exclusionary elements and contents that the ego has erected and which have obstructed the view into higher dimensions.

The enclosed chart at the end of this chapter 'Structure of the human being' corresponds to the micro-and-macro cosmology as outlined in Mandukya Karika by Gaudapada and in the comments of Raphael. It is the spiritual-instrumental structure of the human being in relation to the multilayered inner and outer universes. At a glance we can immediately see a great deal in this chart that normally would take hundreds of books on mysticism and other esoteric doctrines to discover.

The traditional cosmology of the being and the outer worlds contains the purity and clarity of the Vedantic teaching. Cosmos is understood as a fundamental and consistent principle of order that operates equally in the micro-and-macrocosmic parts of creation, in matters large and small, in the universe as in humans. There is order, structure and cosmic law everywhere. There is not a single niche in the limitless worlds of creation without this implicit order and balance. What appears to be chaos at first glance is just a hidden part of order. What do the researchers of chaos theory say on this topic?

> *When we talk about Chaos behavior we do not mean the lack of any order and some completely irregular jumble but – due to the interconnectedness of the many elements, which act with each other and feed back – the unpredictability and incalculability of the nature processes.*[50]

These two researchers make a humble confession: man with his individualized scientific state of consciousness cannot have an overview of the complexity of natural processes nor can he see through them. He can only guess or anticipate that:

> *Behind everything there is one single intention, which often reveals a certain and often hidden meaning, although nobody knows what kind of meaning that is and if one has managed to live that in his life, what was actually intended.*[51]

It would make a huge difference if modern man would reflect on such topics. Who these days seriously asks the question, 'Am I living appropriately, in accordance with my destiny?' Many people live in

---

50 See John Briggs, F. David Peat: Entdeckung des Chaos, (The Discovery of Chaos), Munich, 1990, p. 1 in the introduction by the editor.

51 ibid p. 11, In the book he quotes Joseph Campbell, who paraphrases statements of Arthur Schopenhauer.

a black and white duality. Either they are fatalistic and surrender helplessly to a dubiously staged destiny or they live their days indulgently, without concept, without God, without being embedded into the Whole of nature.

Let us try to characterize the regular individual human being in a matter-of-fact way (as a man). As a baby he cries, as a child he hops and jumps around and plays with his toys (which today are already available in the digitalized form for the super young). As a school kid he carries his books back and forth for years. As a teenager he has to fight his battles with his parents and other authority figures. As an adult he twirls his mustache, fights and quarrels and runs after women. Fame and honor, career and money become the core emphases of his values. He tries to increase his wealth and to hoard it, and he wants to beget children. Then he becomes older and wears glasses and gets artificial teeth inserted. In still later years he wobbles through the landscape using a stick. And then finally he dies.

The moral behind this is: during his short life man makes a little bit of noise on the planet and then he disappears in an instant. Due to the identification with himself as an individual and the illusion of uniqueness he has separated himself from others all his life, in anxious worry about his psychological and material resources. All too often such a life ends in meaningless futility. The common saying that one continues living in his offspring does not help. Is this any kind of consolation? And what happened to my being, to my consciousness, where are my memories, my sense that I am alive, that I am existence? Perhaps in my grandchildren?

As a contemplative intelligent human being one wonders about so much naivety. Or is it perhaps just ignorance or even a crutch for feeling powerless.

Now let us look at the other perspective, which includes the Universal. The difference between the Western man and the Indian-

Hindustani man is quite dramatic. The Westerner sees himself primarily as a physical creature, equipped with a mind in some people's view he even 'possesses' a soul. For the Hindu the human being 'is' primarily soul in his essence and he expresses himself through his psyche, his mind and his body, in order to cope on the physical level. According to this viewpoint the human being lives because he is primarily a soul, because his deepest essence is Atman or the Divine Spirit.

Man's true and only nature is God. Body, mind and soul depend on his soul disposition and not vice versa. When the being begins to come closer to the Divine Spirit he attains security, certainty, perfection, freedom, independence, immortality and eternal blessings. Thus, according to the nature of consciousness, all human beings are actually equal. The same one Atman lies deep within them. These are viewpoints of the Universal, the perspective of the human being that far transcends individuality and allows for a Oneness View. If one, however, looks upon the human being from the aspect of his lower nature with his psyche, ego-sense and intellect, then the individual and the Universal being are seemingly far apart. I like to use an example from my old subject area, electrical science:

The same electricity flows through different kinds of light bulbs and other illuminating objects. But the result of the flow is seen in various diverse ways, in differentiated light and varying degrees of heat. It depends on the lighting equipment chosen (analogue to individual). With the human being it is similar. Depending on his ego-Manas complex, character and temperament, Atman expresses itself very differently. Atman is 'filtered' through these characteristics, and appears very differently, manifesting differentiation, boundary, otherness and individuality.

One could also use a prism as an example to explain it, in which a bright white beam enters and then emerges split into all the colors of the spectrum. Thus man believes that life is full of colors. He has no knowledge of the pure, white beam of light of Atman that occurs before the prism of relativity.

Our mission in life as divine beings is to remove the prism.

To better understand the chart of the structure of human beings presented on page 124f., I take the liberty to quote a longer passage of my Master Raphael from his book: "Advaita Vedanta – Der Weg der Nicht-Dualität" ('Advaita Vedanta – the Way of Non-Duality'), Kamphausen 1998. The chapter deals with the description of coarse matter. We shall then use these explanations as a foundation for other realms of the cosmic fabric, the subtle matter worlds.

> *'All the Eastern and the Western branches of the Tradition agree that the One Being expresses itself on the level of manifestation in different life conditions, in different existential forms or in varieties of ways. One can also say that the Being expresses itself in various vibrational states of consciousness, either on the level of form or formlessness. Therefore, one has to distinguish between the existential realm and the life-forms that live in it or that are in it. Take, for example, the physically dense realm, on which we currently experience our lives; it is an existential level, which consists of solid, liquid and gaseous etc. vibrations even though it belongs to the coarse matter realm (Vaisvanara). In all these vibrational states there are beings that live, move and exist…*
>
> *When the (Mandukya-) Upanishad speaks of Vaisvanara it relates to our physical coarse matter state, of our body, which corresponds with the Universal coarse material plane. It follows that Visva or those beings that identify with Visva make their experiences on one part of the Virat level.*

Visva is the individual being, Virat is the Universal Being. Therefore, Virat is not just our planet but the totality of worlds, which express themselves on the gross matter plane. (p.62 f.)

What we learn here from this example is this: all sheaths of states of consciousness or vibration shown on the left side of the graph have their correspondence on the right side in the Universal realm. Thus the physical sheath corresponds to the Prithiviloka, the sheath of life force (popularly known as astral body) to Kamaloka etc. up to the exalted sheath of bliss with its corresponding Brahmaloka.

With the sheath of the intellect the realms of individuality end. The dashed line indicates the transition to the Universal, starting with the sheath of intellect, the higher intellect, the frequently mentioned Buddhi. The realms of Kamaloka and Manavaloka are worlds (realms) of the lower subtle body. Their degree of vibration is distinctly more refined in the higher worlds of Universal Hiranyaloka and Brahmaloka. In Christian terminology this would refer to the several levels of heaven up to the highest Deity, God, the Father; in Vedanta, Isvara, not to be understood as a person but as a principle.

Raphael explains to us that beings with their light bodies can manifest in all the worlds beyond the physical realm up to Brahmaloka. These worlds are full with those beings. They often stay for eons in different layers, before they have to reincarnate up or down again, according to their Karma. So even in the higher worlds there is still no eternity, only an apparent one, because the time-space components differ greatly from ours here on earth and are different in each level. Recall the length of one day of Brahma from the previous chapter.

After physical death the Jiva, the individualized soul, the reflection of Atman, is guided into one of these realms, according to his vibrational state, his specific characteristics and its energetic capacity. What is wonderful though, is that we do not have to wait for death to come in contact with these planes of existence, but they are always available, just as the different frequency ranges of the radio and television are simultaneously present. Whether we can tune in a station clearly depends on how accurately we can adjust to its physical wavelength.

Great works of artists or brilliant scientists come from the Universal Hiranyaloka realm. Some people are receptive to this very high degree of frequency and are blessed with inspiration in the form of 'seeing' that may possibly be beneficial to all of humanity. To be precise, man cannot invent anything, he can only receive impulses from all that is already existent or manifested in the higher realms or that is lying dormant there as a potential. That should make us humble on the one hand, and on the other hand we should be happy that we can experience such blessings.

Let us summarize: The human being has, by virtue of his birthright of divinity, at all times and on every level of existence the opportunity to be in contact with all the possible frequency levels because his innermost nature as Atman represents all these levels, and all these frequencies are simultaneously present. Therefore the advanced mature aspirant should begin by making his life more spiritual in order to fulfill his one and only goal and Dharma during his lifetime, to recognize himself as the Self, to approach it through qualifications and lastly to fulfill his self-realization in Savikalpa – and Nirvikalpa Samadhi.

As long as we stay in the relative world of individuality, equipped with this ego-mania and never ending stream of thoughts there appears to be a contradiction between the ego-person and Universality.

However, when we experience the first Samadhi, even if only to some degree, or through the Grace of the guru there is a flash of inspiration of higher perspective every possible physical and intellectual understanding changes for this blessed man, as well as the entire view of existence. He becomes God's 'messenger' (?) or better even, he becomes God's likeness on earth, a blessing for others.

At the end of this chapter I'd like to refer to the second part in the chart, that represents the Antahkarana, the totality of the subtle instruments. Without the blessed possession of these inner organs we would not be able to use our five action senses in the physical and psychological realms. The Antahkarana is also the connecting point to the Buddhi that would otherwise be lingering in the Universal, devoid of any possibility to send impulses to the lower nature.

The compact chart is self-explanatory and it is up to the reader to decide in which way, rationally or intuitively, he'd like to understand its contribution to the structure of beings.

Individuality and Universality are two sides of the same coin of the One Atman. Everything is and remains as One. It is not lost, even if it occasionally seems to be the case. Let us for example take Alzheimer's disease as we find it in epidemic proportions affecting the elders in our times. Even this degrading state of consciousness does not alter anything in the eternal memory, which is available to us as Universal beings. Swami Sivananda sums this up beautifully in one of his works:

The body is the quagmire of the soul

The soul is the mover of the body vehicle

When the body is destroyed one day

The spirit remains alive

You continue to have at your command thoughts,

Memory, will power

And the subtle body.

What is so wonderful about Advaita Vedanta is that it not only gives us justified hopes for a meaningful life without illusions, but that it also can convert beliefs and hopes into concrete experiences when practicing its principles, which in intensity and greatness by far exceed our familiar experience.

Aham Brahma Asmi![52]

---

52 One of the Mahavakyas, the four great Mantras, here: I am Brahman!

Structure of the human being

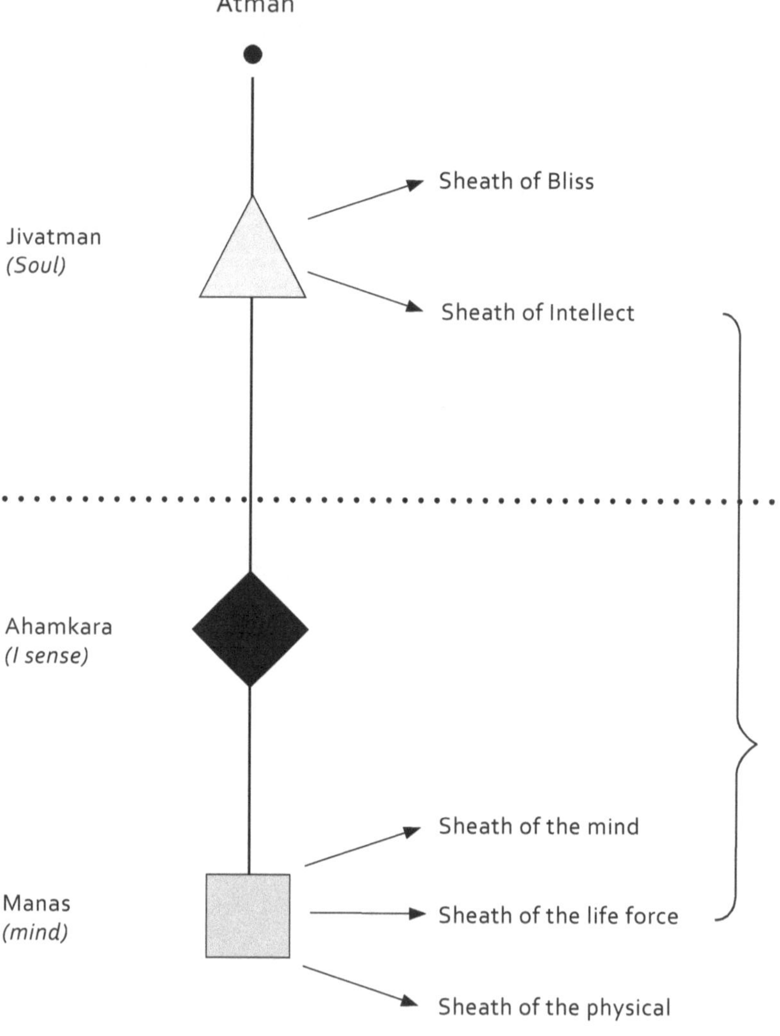

Relativ Planes of Existence

Causal Body
(deep sleep)

Brahmaloka
Highest attainable plane of all forms of existence. Highest Heaven. Isvara and the world oft the Devas (Gods).

Hiranyaloka
Level of the subtle Universal.
World of the Buddhi higher intellect.

Levels of Universality

Levels of individuality

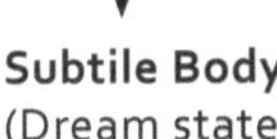

Subtile Body
(Dream state)

Manavaloka
World of the Mind (Intellect)
Level of thinking

Kamaloka
Level of world of wishes, emotions, passions, desirepain;
level of vitality

Physical Body
(state of wakefulness)

Prithiviloka
The physical universe that we perceive with the 5 senses.
Physical world of matter

The ANTAHKARANA
Sukshma Sharira
The Inner Organ
The Subtle Body

The Antahkarana expresses itself as

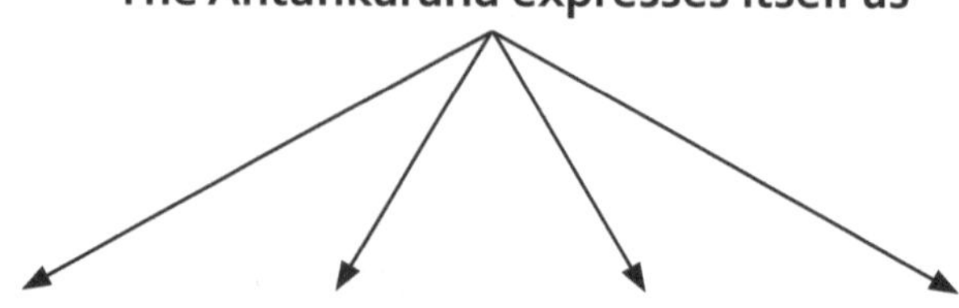

Manas	Buddhi	Ahamkara	Citta
When it takes on the function of weighing up, pros and cons, positives and negatives, analysis. World of thought and science.	When it apprehends and intuitively and directly learns the core truth of things, circumstances and appearances normally hidden to the mind. Transition to universal	When it assumes the function of ego perception of ego-sense, and takes itself for a separate I-subject apart from everything (including God). Ego levels.	When it identifies and unites with an object of desire. Citta is all that man has "inherited" of individual and cosmic predispositions.

11. Significant Changes in the Profile of the Serious Seeker

Botched visions of the future

As a consultant, coach and management trainer, in the 1980s I was often traveling abroad. It was inevitable that I constantly stayed and worked in hotels. Sometimes at night I absorbed foreign energies, which, after I fell asleep used my mind and now and then conjured up from very uncomfortable to outright demonic scenarios. Once, though, something extraordinary happened in sleep at home at the end of a trip. This time it was not a purely intrapsychic projection, but a detailed visionary dream of my future, in which a place where I had stayed overnight and worked rendered up encodings from its energy fields.

I dreamed of long periods of my future in great plasticity and lucid vividness. It was, however, in a highly encoded form, full of symbolism and archetypes. After what I perceived as a long-lasting series of dream events, I awoke briefly with a rather strong feeling of high tension (Eustress). I fell asleep again, and then once again something astonishing occurred: I now dreamed with the same lucidity that the symbols of my dream had dissolved, and I dreamed of their explanations, meanings, of their complete decoding, as if they were the manual for the dream. Then I woke and got up, quickly took my portable cassette recorder (a first generation version) to hand, and recorded both the dream and its interpretation meticulously on tape.

Feeling blessed to now have empirically secured the visions of my future, I slept until the next morning. Who could ever imagine having such a deeply psychological, highly relevant document available to them? I felt blessed.

The next day I wanted to listen to it all over again. In the final count, it was about my own future, and using the knowledge so gained everything could be steered so much better, or so I thought. But I could not find the tape. I turned the house upside down. The tape was gone. But no one had taken it. It never showed up again, and only fragments of the entire sequence of dream events remained in my memory. What sadness enveloped me. First this blessing, then such a pain of loss. And finally one day, much later, the whole scene revealed itself in a flash of comprehension: all three parts of the nocturnal experience – even the recording – was a dream. Dream, decoding and recording.

I then understood one thing thoroughly: between waking (Visva) and dreaming (Sushupta) there is only a tiny difference in the intensity of what is experienced as real. Often none at all. From the standpoint of consciousness our lives are a single unity. And the witness (Atman) is present in all states of consciousness.

This section of the book deals with changes in both the psychological and the spiritual profile of the sincere seeker. Then once again we look more closely at what the goal of Advaita Vedanta is. For this we take a look at Shankara's Atmabodha with the commentary of Raphael[53]:

> *It is not enough to be good in a sentimental way; it is not enough to develop emotional enthusiasm towards transcendence; it is not enough to have a sharp and penetrating mind; required, however, is a 'maturity' of consciousness that arises from a deep 'feel' for the way back home.*

Shankara now puts forward four essential main qualifications. They are aimed at those who:

1. *strive for liberation (Mumuksutva) as the result of 'maturity' and not from avoidance or other such things,*
2. *by means of asceticism (Tapas) have their hearts purified from all thoughts and actions that are not consistent with the Universal 'Dharma',*
3. *have achieved mental stillness (Santanam), after they have brought attraction and aversion, which are characteristic of the ego-sense, under control,*
4. *Have dominated desire-passion (Vitaraginam) for external and internal, material and intangible objects, so that they live in a state of 'dispassion'.*

For Shankara these four qualifications are a prerequisite for understanding-aprehending his work Atmabodha ("Knowledge of the Atman"). As these criteria are not easy to fulfill - to realize them, one needs, as Raphael puts it bluntly, a whole lifetime - this work is just not suitable for beginners. However, for the serious seeker there's no way round these qualifications. At some point, everyone who has been inspired by the Buddhi has to do the work.

---

53 Sankara: Atmabodha, Translation from Sanskrit and Commentary by Raphael, [Publisher] Bielefeld 2009, see pp. 37f.

In his diverse writings Vivekananda, among other things, gives a graphic example on how a student must change his attitude in daily life if he wants to approach God, or even realize Him.

> *A master was bathing in the river with his student. Suddenly the teacher pushed the disciple under water and did not let go. Wildly floundering, gasping for air, the teacher pulled him up again and asked him what he had felt. The student assured him of only one desire: air. Upon the question from the master, whether he had such intense desire for God, the student said no. The Master said in a serious tone: "Develop such a desire for God, then you will reach him."*

This example relates only to the first of Shankara's criteria. But we do not want to be discouraged. Advaita is indeed a very demanding path of highest knowledge, but it is not impossible to follow it. Whoever feels a clear impulse that this path may lead him to liberation, at first could not care less about the qualifications, but just follows the impulse. Everything else will show itself in due time.

Further evidence for the distinct changes in the seeker of truth can be found In the works of the great teachers[54] of modern times. We want to be inspired by their ideas and continue our investigation on the basis of the four major criteria of Shankara.

The maturity demanded by Shankara certainly does not materialize by itself. It is either a gift from past lives, or it will be awakened through an encounter with a mature soul, or even by a sutra from the Shruti. Just the mere fact that the reader is reading a book like this one is a sure sign at the very least of an impending maturity.

---

54 Nikhilananda, Sivananda, Ramakrishna, Vivekananda, Sri Aurobindo, Krishanamurti, Raphael, Ramana Maharshi, Mahatma Ghandi, Sri Yukteswar, HH Sri Bharati Tirta Mahaswamiji, Swami Dayananda, Sri Sri Anandamayi Ma, to name a few.

To strive for liberation is a serious and extraordinarily courageous thing to do. Why? Because there is almost no modern man willing to give up his whole personality. Haven't the teachers, psychologists and psychiatrists drummed into us that we need an intact personality to come to grips with this type of society, to make ends meet? An army of psychotherapists work with so-called disturbed minds, to restore and consolidate the personality. And here comes the Advaitin and demands the dissolution of the personality, indeed, of the whole historical person! Is that not already from the start a psychopathic undertaking, a life-threatening step? It could be interpreted this way from the perspective of the psychological sciences. But what is really behind this divinely inspired counsel? What happens to a man who, thanks to liberation, loses his identification as a person? Is he a candidate for the mental hospital, or do we perhaps not quite understand something with our narrow, limited minds?

The latter is most likely true. We have already emphasized this in this book several times. In the act of liberation the ego-sense (Ahamkara) and the mind (Manas) are sent packing. In the best case, it is a journey of no return. All qualitative features of these characteristics remain untouched, because they are not more than characteristics and in themselves have no independent existence. However, they are integrated into a higher realm, and in advanced students therefore appear as completely new qualities.

It is no longer about mine and thine, about limits and condemnation/rejection, it's about the One View of all, it's about integration and understanding/compassion. The spiritually evolved student appears to think just like any other human being because he speaks, for example. But he no longer thinks with the Manas, instead he transfers his Universal Vision and wisdom directly into his speech, unfiltered by the old conditioning of the lower consciousness and the unconscious. Thus does a Vedantin become such a pleasant human contemporary, because he shows great understanding for the concerns of people.

And usually these students come fully equipped with a "helper syndrome", simply because of their loving hearts for the suffering of our brothers and sisters around the world. If a Wise One helps, it differs from social or altruistically motivated helping. Even the altruistic approach is still hoping for recognition, at least subliminally. The wise student is completely free from these motives. His heart is like the sun: it shines both for the good and the evil, and does not ask anything in return. And anyway, what could we give the sun? It draws its light and strength from itself, similar to the Self in man.

A deeper understanding of the second major qualification of Adi Shankara means asceticism and renunciation. We repeatedly pointed out that this requires no escape into the caves of the Himalayas or the Andes. It's not about any of today's overdone and much-vaunted diets and also not about making the choice between vegetarian, vegan, or even mixed and pure meat diets. With the right attitude you can escape this confusion and consume everything of the boundless variety of food that the Lord has provided for us. In this regard Mahayana Buddhists have developed a very practical, shrewd attitude and guideline. They basically don't eat meat because they cannot kill animals. But if it is already dead, slaughtered by others, they may take and eat this food. Somehow this is a very clever behavior and approach to life. To us Westerners, however, it seems inconsistent.

In Jnana-Yoga/Advaita Vedanta asceticism means only spiritual asceticism: the purification of thoughts, words, emotions and actions. The Vedantin dedicates himself to this difficult piece of work with to the powerful negation mantra: "Neti neti", "not this and not that." Underlying this is the mature insight of the student, that all inner and outer objects that come to him through the senses, including the thoughts, can be not be real, because they come and go, and therefore are contingent and hence not absolute. As long as no real stillness has settled in the mind of the disciple, "Neti neti" is meaningful and makes use of the Shivaic force of dissolution. Only in silence, where subject and object merge, does the mantra lose its meaning and become superfluous. It would not even really bother anyone if it did occur, because it is after all just another thought-form.

A very important hint is also given to us in this second qualifying criterion. Through such asceticism a man's heart is purified. Remember the heart chakra (Anahata). It begins to shine, and so cleanses the lower chakras, and clears the way up to the three higher centers. The effort of spiritual renunciation and asceticism thus opens the door for a glimpse into the Universal. In this way, we meet the demand to become ever more in line with the "Universal Dharma".

Begin and practice it, o seeker:

Movies? Neti neti!
Holiday? Neti neti!
Going out to eat? Neti neti!
Lazy? Neti neti!
Work too much? Neti neti!
Sex? Neti neti!
Internet surfing? Neti neti!
Sports? Neti neti!
Recreation? Neti neti!
Diet and fasting? Neti neti!
Fitness Center? Neti neti!
Family ties? Neti neti!
Social contacts and friends? Neti neti!
Enlightenment? Neti neti!
Self-realization? Neti neti!
Devotion to God? Neti neti!
Yoga? Neti neti!

Now one could argue: OK, stop, then in this case you are no longer still viable in our society, an absolute outsider, a weirdo and an outcast.

Answer: Not at all! I can still do all that, but with the utmost detachment, without attachment, without bond and – Karma Yogically – do it all in the name of God. In the last four examples on our list, we recognize that even such sublime thoughts as enlightenment etc. must be discarded using this mantra – if they are used for a particular purpose with useful effect and for as long as they remain only concepts of Manas. This means anyone who wants to attain enlightenment in order to ... is already in the wrong approach to his meditation, his spiritual practice. Only the unrestricted use of the mantra and a purpose-free attitude coming from deep inside, and without conceptual self-deception, leads to the goal completely by itself, without any effort.

The third qualification Shankara mentions is mental peace. This mainly points to the close-knit interplay of Manas and ego/Ahamkara, the relative, small I. At this stage the advanced student is not interested in either love at first sight or rejection at first glance, neither good nor evil. The student must now work to harmonize all polarities. How can this be done? An illustration: The positive and the negative poles of a battery can release a completely new set of possibilities and synergies through a so-called consumer, say a technical instrument. The energy at rest at the poles is set into a flow by a lamp, for example, and generates light, heat, infrared radiation, etc. If the user is a PC, a thousand different phenomena are created.

In terms of the spiritual approach, we can understand this example so: If we manage to not let ourselves be impressed by the positive or negative poles of bright or dark, light or shadow, love or hate, God or Satan, but with a balanced heart full of kindness, humility and devotion to the Divine, take an attitude of detachment – not indifference (!) – then we will immediately participate in the divine synergy that gives us a foretaste of eternity. We become emotionally more relaxed, physically and mentally calmer, smarter, healthier, more devoted, compassionate, tolerant of frustration, autonomous, independent, inwardly free, outwardly expressing a countenance of friendliness and sympathy. In addition, we leave behind the level of conceptualization in our lives in favor of real knowledge-discernment, we can take clear and groundbreaking decisions, not for self-interest, but for the benefit of all. And finally our mental intelligence gives way to the higher and expresses itself as wisdom.

All of this is a departure. A farewell to the ego and the mind and the thinker. But it is a farewell of a special nature. It ultimately takes place without pain, for that which is given up does not compare with that which is gained. Let us once again use the example of electricity. If we, as the Ego-Manas-Complex being, are comparable to an 80 watt lamp, in the ascended consciousness we are comparable to a lamp of several thousand watts. This comparison also gives us some clarity that the process is about careful, gradual improvement and development. Otherwise, if the cosmic universal energy should come abruptly and in full force, it would explode our small old lamp.

In point four of the qualifications the great Avatara Shankara shows us that we must give up our worlds of wishes (Vasanas). And completely, inside and out. Whoever has dealt with drug-addicted people knows how much a drug addiction literally changes into flesh and blood, manifests in it, and takes its toll. But also these dependencies are not to be underestimated: gluttony, drunkenness, drug addiction, exercise addiction, lethargy, workaholism, leisure and hobby addiction, habit addiction, love addiction, sex addiction and finally even the ego and craving for recognition with its self-love (narcissism).

What is common to all this striving for inner, psychological and material desire? It is addictive. It is a multidimensional instrument of the testing of Maya and holds the Buddhi under control and at a distance, so it cannot just follow through by means of the Antahkarana. Especially with addictions it is tragically clear how much the Jivatman has forgotten itself by its relative identifications in tens of existences. It has permitted a conditioning based on the pleasure-pain principle, which allows seeing only through the spectacles of the individual, although it is part of the Universal (see the diagram for the structure of the human being, page 124). It has put the universal glasses down somewhere and forgotten them. With patience the teacher-master helps to find these glasses again.

We are indeed obliged to further consider and deal with the interior, the exterior, the material and the ideal, but from a new state, that of dispassion. As the word already expresses: addiction, dependence and binding/attachment, desire and passion cause suffering, and bring forth sorrow. One piece of cake is delicious, but with three the stomach goes on strike. For a whole cake you'll need a hospital.

What is too much of a good thing, is too much. Hygiene in the home makes sense. But too sterile a household weakens the immune system and causes disease. Meditation is excellent for calming a too-lively mind, but to want to meditate with pressure and self-imposed compulsion causes the opposite effect, with unrest, an endless stream of thoughts and feelings of not succeeding and failure in spiritual endeavors.

Buddha, the Exalted One, taught the middle way, the way of balance and hence dispassion. This should still inspire us in our spiritual practice of Advaita even today. If we have understood all the instructions and requests of the great teachers, we need to internalize them, assimilate them cognitively, then apply them, and if possible practice mindfulness, serenity, humility and devotion 24 hours a day. The other details of the path of Jnana-self-realization we will learn once we decide to set out on this course and entrust ourselves to an authentic teacher.

Raphael makes no secret of the fact that the Advaita-realization is difficult and therefore only suitable for the few mature. But each of us should check his maturity, his spiritual blocks, just once before he gives up. For many maturity is so familiar that it is not perceived as such. A very important criterion of maturity is the avoidance of Guru-hopping. Many interested people nowadays run from teacher to teacher, from seminar to seminar and await the portentous promise of success from some charismatic leader. But what do they really take away from all this? Mostly concepts, which in their multiplicity often result in utter confusion. The mature soul recognizes his teacher very quickly due to mutual resonance. If this is the case, stay strictly with this teacher, trust and serve him and see in him a divine manifestation who serves the people selflessly.

Don't judge an authentic Guru by his human behavior. If he is a real Guru, this will also show in his moral and ethical attitude and behavior. He sees objects of desire neither in people nor in things or psychic phenomena, but is exalted above all such Samskaras (deep inner impressions) because he has transcended them. He only appears to be the doer. In reality, he is what in Vedanta is called "the doing non-doer". This is the purest Karma Yoga quality.

Remember that it is not only the Master that places his entire existence under the supremacy of the Highest Lord (Isvara). You can and should do it too. If you start with it today, you will soon feel the effects of success: many of the previously mentioned and perhaps somewhat frightening range of qualifications then follow by themselves.

• • •

May the metaphysical knowledge
be liberating and transformative for you;
may it help you
transform the false perspective of the Jiva,
through its connection to the Gunas
to resolve the great error.
May you blaze in the Sacred Fire
and your lower nature
burn to ashes,
so that the Self alone can shine forth.

∞ Shanti Om Tat Sat ∞

12. Jnana-Bhakti – Aphorisms, Poetry, Contemplations

The following lines are not text that should be read like a chapter from a novel, but contemplations that can be reread two or three times, then absorbed in spiritual contemplation, reviewing them in silence.

The texts include elements of both the spiritual yoga (Jnana) and the yoga of love and devotion (Bhakti). They have usually emerged after midnight, when here in the country all around has become quite still; perhaps in the distance an owl calls in mystical seeming sound, or a roebuck barks in the dark forest.

Tips for practice:

A darkened room, a candle, maybe a little incense can help make the contemplation a spiritually elevated moment. In Advaita Vedanta there are no exactly prescribed Asanas (postures). Advanced learners who are able to calm their minds esily can take any comfortable position. Beginners, or those students accustomed to yoga asanas, can sit in a meditation posture on a suitable bench or on pillows.

The back should be straight, the spine its natural anatomical position allowing a relaxed S-shape.

As an effective variant another recommendation is to sit on the bed with your back to the wall and legs crossed. Then read the text, afterwards close your eyes, begin deep abdominal breathing or chest Pranayama, and then allow the text to sink into the spirit as sugar dissolves in hot tea.

After the contemplation simply slide down effortlessly to a reclining position and go to sleep. In this way, the contemplating mind continues to work in the subconscious and causes a movement of energy, which serves to harmonize the chakras. This kind of contemplation is spiritual work on two levels, the conscious and the subconscious.

This type of contemplation is about an aspect of "meditation with object", a dual form of meditation based on the text of a sutra, an image or a spiritual abstraction such as God or all-permeating spirit, etc. Meditation without an object is significantly harder. To this end the student must be able to calm his mind completely - like a lake with a glassy surface.

Sleep

Who rests in sleep?
The body, the feelings, the senses, the mind,
the memory, the desires,
wishes, longings and bonds?

Who exists in sleep?
The body, of which I now know nothing?
The feeling that I do not feel?
The senses that have disappeared?
The mind, which I cannot control?
The memory, which I cannot remember?
The desires, which I do not perceive?
The wishes, too dark to appear?
The longings, melted in the fiery furnace of dissolution?
The bindings, which are all undone
in the rest of sleep?

Who or what exists in sleep?
Nothingness?
It can have no existence, otherwise it would be a something.
The flesh of the body?
Perhaps, but without awareness it is not there.

Just the memory after waking up,
the knowledge,
that I have "slept",
is a gentle hint about something
that all night long stayed awake.
A mystery of consciousness.
Turiya!

Over There

In the illuminated world
in the flight of the soul,
swing the feelings
of lovers,
in the rhythm
of great nature
on this plane of existence.

All earthly worlds
left behind,
floats
the fine bright body
through the luminous universe.

Feelings become objects,
thoughts become reality,
ideas become their own worlds.
Here the soul understands
that it is the Creator
of the inner and the outer.
God in the body,
whether gross or subtle,
always divine;
even though forgotten in earthen life.

The sound of OM
heard as a flute
or ringing bells.
Transformation of original sound
into thousands of variations.
So fine, so beautiful,
that everything since heard
fades against it.

Yin and Yang,
united harmoniously,
innermost interlacing,
polar union,
thus the Light can happen.

Shanti Tat Sat

Secret of Letting Go

Life impression
Impress themselves
In the mind
As if in wax.

The Matrix,
like a wax seal,
remains
until from the
Holy Fire
of a purified mind
it melts.

Before the melting
comes the refining,
before refining, the recognition,
prior to recognition, the will,
before the will, the drive,
before the drive, the impulse,
from within or without.

Blessed is the being,
that receives an impulse.
Woe to the being,

not following the impulse.
Opportunities fly away
as husks in the wind.
Decay and chaos
instead of
growth, maturity and beauty.

O Shankara,
we hear
Your holy warning.

Spiritual Challenge

Under the hard smothering ice
of encrusted demands of life
is located
warm, soft, well-scented,
clear water of
Universal comfort.

The mature Jiva melts it from above,
the water of Buddhi
thaws it from below.

Gentle immersion of the being
in the ocean of life.
Become completely part of That.
Become One, be One.

Tracking down the Self

On the trail of the Self
the purified mind reads
in the impressions
of its past
its old mistakes,
in the presence
its new opportunity.

And before him,
on the unencumbered path
of the future,
he recognizes
the compelling need
to allow the old ruts
in the sands of time
to be freely blown away by the wind.

Only briefly
remain the tracks of the moment
beneath his feet of light.

Step by step,
in perpetual presence
leaving past behind,
the unknown before him, not heeding,
he places his attention
only on the moment of silence.

Emerging assuredness,
surrounded by the holiness
of the inner companions,
completely without a trace.

Life in the Rhythm of the Tradition

Ten Guidelines

1. Balanced Health,
   balanced Sattvic diet, daily exercise in the fresh air, and an alert, reflective, sunny spirit.
2. Prosperity in basic living conditions,
   have sufficient food, drink, sleep, dwelling, finances, social contacts. Purposefulness of living in simplicity.
3. Modesty in desires,
   be satisfied with what is available. Live free of consumer desires. Even scale back on social expectations.
4. Simplicity with no implied superlatives
   in thinking, feeling, acting and throughout life. Simplicity does not mean lack, but to work out for oneself how to deal with given resources responsibly and in moderation.
5. Deep humility towards life and the divine within us,

   be aware every day of the omnipresence of the Divine, be grateful for the gift of life experience, trust one's life to God without intervention of the mind (Bhakti and Karma Yoga).
6. Beauty of the human being,
   recognize the true beauty hidden within us, and radiate it out as well as one is able. The face of the truly spiritual man is the face of God. God is pure aesthetics, both inside and out. The "Beauty in Itself" comes from divine wisdom. It is "Sophia".
7. Platonic Eros
   Eros, according to Plato, is the natural, vibrant fabric of love between God and man, and between people. Regardless of whether it is physical, emotional or energetic in vibration. Higher emotional sense, expression of pure love and bliss. A universal Ananda aspect. Independent of externality.

8. High dignity in dealing with each other and more generally as an attitude.
   Absolute trust in each other in marriage, friendship, partnership. Dignity towards sensual seductions by third parties. Recognition of the other as myself. Renunciation of revenge, infliction of pain and suffering. I see you as myself. How could I wish myself harm? Clarity, openness, trust, authenticity, maturity, credibility, detachment and especially devotion to the Divine lead to dignity.
9. Spirituality as a yogic practice and approach to life,
   come to deeper inner calm through the presence of I AM, mindfulness of the thinker and the thoughts and meditation, with and without an object, depending on the possibilities. Yoga means union or reunion with the Divine. This is the highest human goal.
10. Holy Fire as a "living peace" in our hearts,
    be pervaded by the kindness and love of the divine power. It emanates from the Maha-Atma Isvara and our hearts are the prism and the center of accumulation for it. All the energy that can lead to reunification collects here. At the end point we realize: I am He. Soham!
    Walking the path of fire means: burn everything, the whole person, all essences of old karma. Once ignited, the fire is always on, always blazing, unstoppable, until the essence is fully purified and becomes something else, something higher. Persona, ego and Manas are burned. A final metamorphosis takes place. This fire burns all the strife and turmoil to ashes. Only now is real peace possible, however, it is not a static peace but a "living peace".

Do you have the initial knowledge and the courage and the strength for the weighty undertaking of such a ten-step path? Do you want to favor the Holy instead of the profane while standing in the middle of life and being in the world, and simultaneously perform your duties (for the true aspirant does not flee the world!) Then you can succeed.

O seeker after truth, embark on this path and become reborn in the sense of a primal baptism. Whoever walks the Path of Fire earnestly, steadily and full of devotion and humility, will see God as

Aham Brahma Asmi

I am Brahman!

Balancing Act

Questioner (Q): Should one then not laugh or cry?

Answer (A): Both are just ordinary, human characteristics from the repertoire of default emotions. But what usually follows one or the other?

Q: Well, often the opposite of the previous one.

A: In this always constant change the being swings back and forth in the swirl of his mostly uncontrolled emotionality. Would not it be useful to obtain a certain balance?

Q: Yes, of course, but if you suppress feelings, repress them, then they jam up, which can lead to big problems.

A: It's not about repression, but about equalizing, balancing. Laugh and let go, cry or be sad and release. And all within an appropriate timeframe.

Q: What is a reasonable time? A day, a week?

A: Before excessive euphoria sets in, which can lead to unreal thinking and can evoke an equally strong reverse reaction, or before depressive states set in. In both cases, before suffering is felt, this is the appropriate time period.

Q: But if I am happy, I won't be suffering.

A: Not directly, but in a world based on duality suffering happens in the wake of joy. Nothing can exist without its opposite.

Q: Isn't that a totally bland life, without any extremes?

A: Who asks themselves this?

Q: Well, I, I myself with my ability to reflect.

A: Who is this me, it is the same as the ability to reflect?

Q: No, it's my thinking.

A: We are faced with a basic problem of human nature. The ego is not the thinking, the thinking is not the ego. But both work together and jointly assess processes of life from the perspectives they hold to be true. Getting back to the original question of whether life is bland and boring without strong polarities .... The socially normalized idea holds that this is probably so, but on closer knowledge of the being, we note that it is the Gunas (passions) that make us believe this. If we have mastered the Gunas, then we control the thinking and feeling. The wise man always lives beyond the gunas, without them being able to touch him. He perceives joy and sorrow, without being affected by them. The entry point is reached via the higher Sattva Guna.

Q: So a kind of neutral? How awful!

A: No, certainly as an alive being, but unaffected by duality. The wise man is immersed in the divine Ananda, in which all states are available. Pure awareness. Only in this way can the action take place in complete balance.
The serious novice (one on the Way), can realize this step by step.

Carpe Diem

The Yin in Yang,
the Yang in Yin,
so goes the day
with sense in it then.

Opening

Once the mature heart wide open
the gods can praise
the blessing will come
from above
then.

Night Mantra

Insistently gold green
glimmers the spherical round
of a rising full moon.
Cool freshness encloses the skin.
The call of the screech-owl from afar
is a chanting to the moon
who, with a pale white smile
replies in silence.

The mantra of the night,
evocation of silence,
surrounds all,
every being permeated
with its soft power,

an atonal vacuum
contains all sounds as seed
the audible and the
deeply hidden.

O divine sound
of a wonderful magic night.
But only the disenchanted soul
might hear your vibration
that leads
to the immeasurable kingdom
of eternity.

Luminous

Life is light, not darkness.
Clarity, not mist,
expanse, not narrowness.

With our lives
we must provide
a perfect platform
so that the high-flying
Angels of bliss
Have a place to land.

The New Life

The seeker touched by fire
knows why he uses his power.
Has life itself not lead him
to this brand new situation?

Are not the tracks of his past shut down,
and at their end,
where the grass of the past grows
over sleeper and steel,
a new switching shunt installed
where the old hard strands
finally give up
and take a new direction?

He leaves his old Home[55],
that he had made
through many years
many lives.

But is it not also
the unfriendly refuge
for much suffering
and memories,
that urgently need
to be cleaned
by the powerful mind?

---

55 The Ego-Manas complex and the identification with it.

This new chance in life
may seem at the beginning
to work diffusely,
but already carries the taste
of honey-sweet knowledge.

Why?
Because from now on
he can lead a life
so informed
by such great possibility of knowledge
that one may normally only acquire
after seemingly endless successions
of earthly lives.

He still fears a little
to abandon the familiar,
but how can one fear
the very life
that carries and upholds one?

Man fears God,
who dwells within him
without his knowledge.
Since the dawn of life
man has also feared
himself.
Could there be anything
more paradoxical?

In the alienation
from pure being
lies hidden all the suffering in the world.

Fourteen Points of Mindfulness

1. Take care with whom you surround yourself,
2. Be mindful of whom you trust,
3. Be mindful of who and what you emotionally get involved with,
4. Give heed to the internal before the external,
5. Pay attention to your growing discrimination (in all aspects of life)
6. Pay attention to your detachment and serenity,
7. Be mindful of your feelings,
8. Be mindful of your thoughts moving in grooves,
9. Watch your desires (particular tendencies),
10. Watch your pride,
11. Be mindful of yourself as a person
12. Watch your self-image,
13. Be mindful of your inner guide,
14. Be mindful of the truth behind everything.

Spiritual Botany

We are the buds
of a flower still closed,
one which must still bloom.
Once the sun shines down upon it
from the rooted depths
the nectar of life ascends,
and it unfolds all by itself.

Isvara, Maya, Samsara,
this is Nature!

Glossary

The world famous Indian guru Sathya Sai Baba once wonderfully defined the meaning of the Sanskrit language:

"Sanskrit is an immortal language;

her voice is eternal;

her call echoes through the centuries.

Embedded in her is the basis

for all languages of the world."

In this glossary, we use the simplified, transliterated inscription of Devanāgarī, the most commonly used Sanskrit font in India. It contains only three special characters. They are the stretched vowels ā, ī and ū, each with a line over it to distinguish them clearly from the short-spoken vowels a, i and u.

For the Sanskrit lay-person this is completely sufficient for the unique identification of the original word, and makes for an easier readability. In the ancient times of the exclusively oral tradition only the exact pronunciation and the related sound vibration were used.

Advaita: Not-twoness, non-duality, the One-without-Second.

Advaita Vedānta: The Vedanta of non-duality systematized by Shankara. A theory of knowledge, in which the world is experienced directly as Brahman, beyond illusion and duality.

Ācharya: Spiritual teacher, master. He lives the teaching.

Axial Age: According to Karl Jaspers, the period from 800-200 BC. A time period in which a religious spiritualization takes place in four different cultural regions of the world independently and simultaneously, and which gave rise to great changes in the human condition.

Advaitin: Colloquially, a follower of Advaita Vedanta; an actualized teacher / master.

Ahamkāra: The I-sense, the sense of self, the ego, part of the psychic entity (Antahkarana).

Anāhata: Heart Chakra; in Advaita one of the most important chakras.

Antahkarana: Internal Organ; complex functional structure of the psyche.

Archetype: According to CG Jung, prototypical images, energy-rich primordial symbols anchored in the collective unconscious.

Āsana: seat; posture in yoga.

Ashtāngayoga: Eightfold path of the Yoga of Patanjali, completed in Samadhi.

Aspirant: candidate of a spiritual path.

Ashram/Āsrama: domicile of a holy or wise man; the four stages of life described in the Veda, Brahmacharya, Grihasta, Vanaprastha and Samnyāsa. Ashram is also called the solitude of the forest, in which the family father together with his wife retires in the fourth stage of life.

Ātmabodha: a work of Shankara, describing the awakening to the reality of the Self.

Ātman: The hidden foundation of being, the true self, the identity of man with God (Brahman).

Avatāra: The descent, the appearance of God on earth. He passes through birth and life without karmic consequences, alone in free will. Examples are Rama, Krishna, Buddha, Christ.

Avidyā: Ignorance, lack of wisdom, darkness of ignorance; consequence of Maya.

Bhagavān: The Exalted, God in human form revealing His unlimited fullness.

Bhakta: Devotee of God, devotion-filled worshiper of God; practitioner of the Bhakti Yoga path.

Bhakti: Adoration, unconditional love of God, intimate union of these.

Brahmaloka: One of the highest relative levels of existence; the world of the gods.

Brahman: The nameless, formless, all-encompassing, eternal, absolute, cannot be experienced with the senses or mind, it reveals itself in Samadhi.

Brahmasūtra: collection of writings of the Vedanta philosophy, probably written by Vyasa. Important basic scriptures of Vedānta, also called Vedāntasūtra.

Buddha: The Awakened; term for the historical Buddha, Prince Gautama Siddhārta.

Buddhi: Also Buddhi Viveka, higher discriminatory power, higher intellect; placed over the lower intellect Manas (mind); superconscious intuition.

Burn-out syndrome: Chronic fatigue syndrome, very common in contemporary Western society, often coupled with a crisis of purpose-existential crisis.

Cakra; Cakras: Chakras are subtle energy centers, which are penetrated by subtle and gross material-physical forces and mutually influence each other.

Codifier: In Vedanta terms an enlightened Master who can "decode" the scriptures of the Vedas or the Upanishads and convert their symbolic content into understandable language by virtue of his awakened, Universal Mind.

Citta: Perception and thought only arise from Citta, the subtle basis of the spirit, mind.

Dakshināmūrthi: name for Shiva as the supreme teacher and preceptor of the people, and also the Gurus, Yogis and Masters.

Dattātreya: A World Teacher, saints and sages of ancient times; is considered part of the incarnation of the Trinity of Brahma, Vishnu and Shiva.

Devanāgarī: The normal Sanskrit script.

Dharma: God's command, order, or law; following the dictates of conscience and inner voice; duties and responsibilities of a spiritual seeker, his destiny because of his karma.

Dhyāna: Meditation, contemplation, inner immersion, internalization; Dhyāna can lead to Samadhi; seventh limb in the eightfold path of Raja Yoga.

Ego-Manas Complex: (also Ego-Manas alliance) the close interaction of the Manas with the Ahamkara; I-thinking, often leading to the involvement of the small I with the psyche and world.

Emergence: The Emergence (from the Latin emergere-ascend) is the spontaneous, often inexplicable emergence of new properties or structures of a system as a result of the interaction of its elements. It simply happens, cannot be forced.

Gaudapāda: Paramguru of Shankara; author of the Mandukya Upanishad comments, along with Shankara considered to be the founder and codifier of Advaita Vedanta and Asparsa Yoga.

Gnosis: Theory of knowledge, religions research term for various religious teachings. Roots in the 2nd- 3rd century AD, partly earlier.

Govindapāda: Name of the student of Gaudapada, Master of Shankara.

Guna: The three Gunas Tamas, Rajas and Sattva are fundamental forces of the primeval nature "Prakriti", the entire phenomenal world of Maya appears from them. In order to achieve realization the Gunas must be brought into balance.

Guru: Analogous for "destroyer of darkness". As spiritual master the Guru leads the disciple into the light, he knows all the dangers and obstacles.

Hatha Yoga: Hatha Yoga is a specialized variant of Raja Yoga, known as the Yoga of effort and body postures (Āsanas).

Hedonism: Highest expression of sensual lusts and pleasures; basically an egotistically oriented lifestyle.

Highest Guru: This refers to the cosmic Guru, the Avatar, the perfect incarnation of God on the subtle and coarse-material levels.

Initiation: An initiation into the small or great mysteries of Eastern and Western Traditions. The Master or Guru gives it as a transcendental act to the mature student who has the appropriate qualifications.

Intelligible: In Plato's theory, there are objects that are not accessible to the world of sense, and they can be detected only through the mind-intellect. The intelligible world is considered superior to the physical world.

Īshvara: Ruler, almighty lord of creation, God in manifested form, the personal God who is worshiped in all religions under different names; in the Vedānta Saguna Brahman, Brahman with attributes.

Jagadguru: World Teacher, he fulfills a universal task for all beings.

Japa: Reciting a holy name or mantra; a form of meditation with object.

Jivanmukta: A human being who has experienced liberation, enlightenment in his lifetime. A free being in all the gross and subtle planes of existence.

Jivatman: The individualized self, a reflection or ray of Atman, but identical with it; in religion science the soul.

Jnāna: Knowledge, wisdom, understanding, spiritual insight; as super-conscious knowledge it makes the knowledge of all the relative superfluous.

Jnāna Yoga: One of the four main yogas, yoga of highest knowledge, which leads to the realization of Brahman.

Jnāna Yogi: One who consistently walks the Jnana Yoga path.

Jnānin: A sage, one who is free, who sees only "the Supreme Lord" in all, that has experienced the unity of Truth on which all universes are based.

Kabbalah: Mystical tradition of Judaism with roots in the Torah. Most important scripture of K. is the Zohar; The K. also contains Gnostic, Neo-Platonic and Christian elements.

Kāla: Dark time, the god of time, or even Yama, the god of death.

Kali Yuga: The Iron or Dark Age, in which we currently live; it began in 3102 BC and is supposed to last 432,000 years. Social life, and especially family cohesion falls apart, the ego-principle prevails; brutality, corruption and aggression gain the upper hand.

Kāma-Manas: A powerful aspect of Manas, "home" of the wishes and desires, of appetites, pleasure-pain center such as grief-joy.

Karma: Karma or Karman has very diverse meanings; here used as a cause-and-effect principle, the sum of all actions in this or in previous existences. Control authority for the kind of rebirth.

Krishna: Name of a perfect incarnation of God, an Avatar of Vishnu, and is said to have lived in the transition period to the Kali Yuga around 3100 BC, in India. The Bhagavadgita documents his universal teachings to Arjuna and forms the basic work of Advaita Vedanta.

Krishnamurti: Jiddu Krishnamurti (1895-1986), world-renowned Indian author, theosophist and spiritual teacher.

Kriya Yoga: A form of Raja Yoga, called the yoga of practical effort; became popular through Paramahansa Yogananda and his teacher Sri Yukteswar. Today courses are offered through the Self Realization Fellowship, USA and Europe.

Lao Tzu: "Old Master", a legendary Chinese philosopher and sage believed to have lived in the 6th century BC; author of the Tao Te Ching.

Loka: Space, world, level, universe; In Vedanta Loka is used to divide the hierarchical world layers, the gross and subtle levels.

Maha Atma: Also Mahat, the universal spirit, synonymous with Īsvara.

Maharishi Mahesh Yogi: Often abbreviated to Maharishi; popular Indian spiritual teacher (1918-2008), also known as Guru of the Beatles. Founder of Transcendental Meditation.

Mahāsamādhi: Complete experience of the absolute Reality in the transition to physical death. A spiritual master does not die in the conventional sense, but changes levels of existence with full awareness.

Mahavakya: term for the four major Vedic tenets, which affirm the identity of the human Self with Brahman; eg Aham Brahma Asmi (I Am Brahman).

Mahayuga: A great cycle consisting of the four world ages or yugas.

Manas: The relative mind, empirical mind, the thinking organ, the sixth sense; also means psyche; in Manas all sensory input is collected, coordinated and processed, and then submitted to the higher discriminatory capacity of the Buddhi.

Māndūkya-Upanishad: Upanishad of the Atharvaveda; mostly about the importance of OM and the four states of consciousness. Gaudapada wrote his famous Karika (commentary) about it.

Maya: Maya works within the human, relative consciousness with two main forces: projection and deception-illusion. But it is also the actual creative force of Īsvara. As a phenomenon of consciousness it expresses itself in humans as imperfect perception, not-knowing. Nonetheless, this cosmic illusion is part of the reality of God.

Moksha: Freedom, liberation, salvation; the being ultimately achieves liberation from duality and rebirth. Through Moksha, the circle of evolution of all previous incarnations closes. The being has found its way back to its origin. It is the highest achievable goal in life.

Mumuksutva: The sincere pursuit of liberation.

Neoadvaitin: Representative of a modern doctrine of often highly simplified partial aspects of Advaita Vedanta.

Neti neti: A mindfulness exercise in Advaita Vedanta, in which all attempts to describe Brahman in relative terms is conducted ad absurdum: "Not this, not this!"

Nihilism: Philosophical doctrine of Nothing (Latin: nihil). Final non-existence of all that is concrete and imaginary as well as the transcendental. Vedanta rejects Nihilism, because nothing can arise from nothing, as Shankara puts it. Not to be confused with the

Vedantic “emptiness” or the term “Shūnyatva”, these are concepts of emptiness, which carry the meaning of “full of potential”.

Nirguna Brahman: The formless and featureless Brahman; experience of Unity.

Nirvikalpasamadhi: Samadhi without sensory impressions; highest transcendental state of consciousness.

Nisargadatta Maharaj: also called Sri Nisargadatta Maharaj (1897 to 1981), was a cigarette vendor in Bombay, seen by many Indians as an enlightened master. Based on the Advaita Vedanta, he taught in a simple, understandable language.

Noûs (Greek): The highest intelligence, superior or pure intellect, the highest mind.

OM: AUM: A symbol, a mantra, a “description” that comes closest to the Absolute Brahman. In a “mature soul” enduring recitation of the seed syllable OM or AUM, can lead to liberation.

Orphism: A cosmology and soul teaching; (approx. 6th-5th century BC), which goes back to the mythical Greek poet-singer Orpheus. Their main aim was to prepare for an expected survival of the soul after the death of the body.

Osho: A very popular Indian philosophy professor (1931-1990) and founder of the Neo-Sannyas movement. He had various names, most recently called Osho. He taught and practiced a synthesis of Indian philosophy and Western psychotherapy.

Paradigm: Term for a certain scientific school of thought (since the 18th century), mindset or type of belief.

Paramahansa Yogananda: Great spiritual teacher (1893-1952); he was considered Premavatar, a divine incarnation; he made Kriya Yoga, which is considered part of Raja Yoga, very well known.

Parmenides: One of the most important pre-Socratic philosophers in the 6th-5th Century BC. His teaching is an example of a Western tradition, which at its core is identical with the teachings of the Indian Vedanta.

Patanjali Maharshi: Author of the Yoga Sutras, the founder of Yoga. When he lived is unknown.

Plato: Greek Philosopher (428/427-348/347 BC), one of the most influential people in the history of thought; his epistemology, metaphysics, and cosmology have many parallels and similarities to the Vedanta.

Plotinus: founder and most renowned representative of Neo-Platonism (205-270 BC). As the focus of his philosophical deliberations he saw the approach to the Platonic "One Good", which he understood as a fundamental principle of all reality, as the superconscious experience of union with the One. For the Advaitin this is identical with Brahman.

Prakriti: Primal nature, primordial matter out of which fine and coarse material universes are made; from the earth to the world of gods, she uses her three Gunas as properties and basic forces for the diverse manifestations of the universes.

Prāṇāyāma: Yogic breath regulation that harmonizes the Prana, the life force.

Psyche: (Greek: psyche, life force, soul) In scientific psychology psyche means soul or soul-life, concerning the inner being of man; in Vedanta, this is further refined, here it is only an inanimate instrument which the Jivatman (the individual soul) uses for its existence in the world of forms and manifestations.

Purana: literary genre; description of ceremonies and festivals as devotional worship of the personal deity; the Puranas belong to the classical holy scriptures; reports on the working of the Divine (Īshvara) on earth.

Pythagoras: Greek philosopher (570-510 BC) and pre-Socratic mathematician, scientist and founder of a major religious and philosophical school (Pythagorean), which among other things, dealt with the transmigration of souls.

Raja Yoga: One of the four main yogas, in addition to Jnana, Bhakti and Karma Yoga, also known as royal yoga; founder or Codifier was Patanjali (Yoga Sutras).

Rama: Avatar of Vishnu, a divine incarnation; after him came Krishna; the life story of Rama is enshrined in the Ramayana, author of which was Valmiki.

Ramakrishna: Significant Bengali saint (1836-1886); a great Bhakta, he emphasized the inner unity of religions and that with sincere practice all would lead to enlightenment.

Ramana Maharshi: Indian saint (1879-1950); he referred the seeker always to the true self (Ātman) and recommended Vicāra as a useful method, eg to ask: "Who am I?"

Raphael: A contemporary European Master, who teaches the unity of One Tradition of East and West. Extensive literature on Advaita Vedanta, Kaballah, Orphism, Yoga paths, Plato, the Path of Fire and the Master-Student dialogue; lives completely withdrawn in a hermitage.

Sadhana: General term for the different and sincerely performed spiritual practices of the various Yoga Teachings.

Saguna Brahman: Brahman with attributes; Ishvara is the first manifestation of Saguna Brahman; from here appears all creation in all universes and planes of existence.

Samādhi: experience of unity as pure consciousness; endpoint of all meditations; it cannot, however, be striven for, demanded or approached methodologically.

Samkalpa: Fixed determination, willpower, controlled, self-willed streams of thought.

Samsāra: Describes the world of becoming as a perpetual cycle; Man experiences repeated birth and death as a natural process of worldly life, which can only be ended by liberation.

Sanskrit: English form for Samskrita, the Sanskrit language, is considered as a subtle form of language, primarily suitable for describing spiritual reality, less so for the material. Saraswati, wife of Brahma, the creator god of the Trimurti, is considered to have gifted it to man.

Sanātana Dharma: The eternal religion, eternal law, eternal order; the timeless truth that was revealed to the Rishis (seers).

Sarasvati: Also Saraswati, goddess, consort of Lord Brahma; goddess of fluency, of learning, of intuition and of the Arts; The origin of Sanskrit is attributed to her as well.

Satsanga: Accumulated strength of a community of serious spiritual aspirants; good company, proper dealings, spiritually conducive; mutual inspiration in the presence of a qualified Teacher, Master, Guru.

Sattva: Being, existence; among the three Gunas Sattva is the highest; balance in life habits; gateway to the Universal.

Savikalpasamādhi: Fusion of subject-object relations, but there still remains a slight trace of duality, which is fully dissolved in Nirvikalpasamādhi.

Student qualifications: The most important are Viveka (higher discriminatory power), Vairagya (mental renunciation, detachment, stable composure) and an unquenchable thirst for liberation.

Self: Popular, modern term for the soul, in the Vedanta, it is Ātman; goes far beyond the psychic; the divine essence or spark in man.

Shankara: One of the greatest saints and philosophers of India; Codifier of Advaita Vedanta.

Shankara Matha: Mathas in India founded by Shankara, places of knowledge, Vedantic monasteries.

Shankara-ācārya: Originally "the master Shankara"; the title for great teachers that preside over the lineage of Shankara in the Mathas.

Shanti: A collective term for very important qualities such as inner peace, calmness, equanimity, peace with oneself and the world and God, the suspension of the senses and passions.
Salutation between teachers/masters and students.

Shivaic Resolution: In Advaita Shiva is a central deity of the Trimurti, because only with the help of his power of dissolution can the ego and the entire lower nature of man be overcome, dissolved, and transcended; this leads to a complete renewal of the liberated being.

Shruti: The hearing and the heard; in ancient Vedic times it was the only form of transfer of pure knowledge; term for the scriptures of the Vedic tradition; direct expression of divine revelation, therefore, the Shruti has absolute authority.

Siddhi powers: Described by Patanjali as paranormal abilities that can develop in a yogi in the course of his efforts; in Yoga they are counted as normal and natural, albeit for earthly life, unusual powers.

Smirti: Writings from memory; similar to the Sruti the writings of the Smirti are also considered sacred; although they are written by people, they stabilize the remembrance of the Holy Tradition.

States of consciousness: in Vedanta they are mainly described as being four: waking, dream, deep sleep and the so-called Fourth, Turiya, the Superconscious

Sutra: Verse, aphorism, guidelines, rules for spiritual development.

Swami Dayananda Saraswati: A contemporary world-renowned Swami, authority of Advaita Vedanta; founder of some Āsramas in India and the United States.

Swami Sivananda Saraswati: (1887-1963) was a well known Yoga master and great teacher of Vedanta, founder of the "Divine Life Society" and the "Yoga Vedānta Forest Academy"; he taught the "Yoga of Synthesis", the unification of four great yogas.

Tapas: Spiritual practice, discipline, asceticism, that can produce the higher spiritual energetics.

Tat Tvam Asi: One of the four major Mahvakyas; "That (Divine Self) You Are!"

Transformation: Higher development/ascent of consciousness; reaching another level of existence; advanced spiritual qualities or qualifications.

Trimurti: The three aspects of one divine reality in the Saguna Brahman, Brahma, Vishnu, Shiva as creator, preserver, destroyer/ renewer.

Upādhi: Veiling, addition, body shell; man has five main Upādhis, corresponding in their vibration to the respective cosmic levels.

Upanishad: Sitting at the feet of the Master, to receive the highest teachings; class of sacred writings belonging to the Shruti and explaining the completion and the essence of the Vedas in nuanced detail.

Vairāgya: to achieve distance and growth out of the transitory things of relative reality; detachment, calmness, dispassion.

Vaisvanara: The waking state of man, one of the four states of consciousness.

Vedanta Teacher: In the classical Advaita (not Neo-Advaita) a disciple of a Master who exhibits qualifications beyond those of the student, such as anchorage in Being, spiritual authenticity, the Teaching in the foreground instead of his person, living the principles of Realization; a calling to be a Teacher by a Master of Sacred Tradition by virtue of his specific Dharma.

Vedāntin: representative of the Vedānta; a qualified, sincere follower of this path of realization.

Vedas: Sanskrit - veda, from vid (see), knowledge, highest spiritual knowledge; designation for the entirety of the oldest historical texts of Indian literature; considered an elucidation of eternal reality, not created by man, but "seen" by Rishis.

Vicious circle: A seemingly inescapable situation in which cause and effect of a situation reinforce each other and result in a repeating loop.

Vidyā: Wisdom, knowledge; superconscious knowledge, spiritual, intuitive experience.

Vishnu: The sustainer of creation, the all-pervasive, the omnipresent; one of the three of god aspects of the Trimurti.

Viveka: Mental clarity, stronger discriminatory power as an aspect of Buddhi; differentiation, eg; between the true and the untrue, real and non-real; important qualification for the serious aspirant of Vedanta.

Vivekachudamani: "Crown jewel of the power of discrimination", a foundational work of Advaita Vedānta, attributed to Shankara.

Vivekananda: "The bliss of discrimination", the name of the main student (1863-1902) of Ramakrishna, who, unlike his guru, has emphasized and lived more the Jnana aspect than the Bhakti; an eloquent Swami.

Vyasa: Complier, also known as Vedavyasa (codifier of the Vedas), a mythical sage, complier of important ancient Indian writings; regarded as the initiator/founder of the Vedānta.

Yama: God of Death, directs and commands souls according to their Karma, provides for cosmic balance.

Yoga: General term for the (re)union with the divine through exercises, practices, and consistent discipline.

Yogasūtra: Name of the formulations of Patanjali, founder of the eightfold path (Ashtanga), wherefrom Raja Yoga

Yogin (m): Yogini (f): People who practice yoga and place their lives in the service of the Supreme.

Yuga: Generation, world-era; the four Yugas of Satyayuga, Tretayuga, Dvāparayuga and Kaliyuga, a total of 4,320,000 human years; the divine Dharma decreases steadily in the order of the Yugas; in the Kali Yuga especially there appear Avatars to stand by to help the people, to leave them the eternal Truth in speech and writing.

OM TAT SAT